TALES FROM THE
VICARAGE

Good Luck for
The Trial James!

Best Wishes

Tom~~~

TALES FROM THE VICARAGE

A collection of writing inspired
by Watford Football Club

Volume Four by Lionel Birnie

TALES FROM
www.talesfrom.com

First published in Great Britain in 2015
by Tales From

Printed and bound by SS Media

ISBN 978-0-9932381-0-9
Jacket illustration by Simon Scarsbrook

Tales From Ltd
2 Gaddesden Lane, Redbourn, St Albans, AL3 7NP
Registered company number: 9082738

www.talesfrom.com
info@talesfrom.com

TALES FROM THE VICARAGE

CONTENTS

ABOUT THE AUTHOR

Lionel Birnie is a journalist, author and Watford supporter. He began his career at the *Watford Observer* in 1993 before specialising in cycling. He first covered the Tour de France in 1999, writing for *Cycling Weekly* and *Cycle Sport*. In 2008, he began covering cycling for *The Sunday Times*. The 2015 Tour was the 13th he has worked on as a journalist.

His first book about Watford Football Club was *Four Seasons,* a glossy, hardback book featuring photographs by Alan Cozzi telling the story of Graham Taylor's second spell as manager between 1997 and 2001.

In 2010, Lionel founded Peloton Publishing and wrote *Enjoy the Game,* which tells the story of the most remarkable decade in Watford's history. The book documents the rise from the Fourth Division to the top flight, Europe and the FA Cup final and is based on dozens of exclusive interviews with former players and staff.

The 100 Greatest Watford wins, Lionel's third book about the Hornets, was published in 2011, and the following year he started the *Tales from the Vicarage* series.

He also devised *The Cycling Anthology,* a collection of books about professional cycling and ghosted autobiographies for top cyclists Sean Kelly and Rob Hayles. Lionel is also one of the co-owners and hosts of The Cycling Podcast.

Find out more online:
lionelbirnie.com
talesfrom.com
cyclinganthology.com
thecyclingpodcast.com

INTRODUCTION

BY THE EDITOR

When the first volume of this series was published in the autumn of 2012, the Pozzo era was in its infancy. There was optimism but also some scepticism at the transformation that had happened in such a short space of time during that summer. Laurence Bassini had gone and the club's financial future was no longer hanging by a thread, but Sean Dyche had also been removed and the jury was still out on Gianfranco Zola. Would he understand the demands of the Championship, or were we witnessing a repeat of the disastrous Gianluca Vialli experiment?

There was a chapter in volume one of *Tales from the Vicarage* called The Italian Job, Part One which was intended to serve as a warning from history not to get too carried away too soon.

Certainly I was sceptical to begin with. Results were hit and miss and performances were hesitant. Early home defeats to Ipswich, Bradford in the Capital One Cup and Brighton did little to discourage me from feeling that the new additions were unsuited to the challenge. A 5-1 thrashing at Derby had me fearing the worst.

The question I could not lodge from my mind was this: why would successful business people want to own a mostly loss-making football club in a medium-sized English town?

The goal, of course, was to reach the Premier League, not just for a fleeting visit but to establish the club among the top ten or 12 in the country, and reap the rewards of membership of the richest league in the world. Here we are, three years on, and the first major goal has been achieved. Watford have gained automatic promotion to the top flight for only the second time in their history.

Earlier this summer, while I was covering the Tour de France, I bumped into Paolo Tomaselli – an Italian journalist who covers cycling in July and Serie A during the football season. Paolo knows the Pozzos well because he watches Udinese regularly, and in volume two of this series he wrote a brilliant chapter explaining their business background, football history and motivations.

'What about Watford, eh?' he said as we stood in some corner of France. 'I knew they would make it to the Premier League sooner rather than later. Now we'll see how good the Pozzos are.'

The transformation in the club's fortunes in three short years seems remarkable. Back when I was writing and editing volume one of this series, it felt almost like therapy. There had been so much uncertainty about the club's financial future, so many brushes with potential disaster and so many times that we had been forced to watch as our best players were sold on to keep the wolf from the door, that the past felt like the safest place to be.

But in all the excitement to embrace the future, it can sometimes be forgotten that a football club's past is the thing that binds us all together. Whether young or old, we all remember our first match, our first hero and the great days that bring a smile to our lips when things are not going so well.

Hopefully this series of books has given you cause to reflect and smile as it has grown into an eclectic collection of writing. Each volume has been slightly different, and for this fourth edition I have gone solo with ten stories that appealed to me.

There is a mix of the past and the present, and plenty to set the club's latest achievements in some sort of historical context.

And as this collection has come together it has struck me yet again just how interwoven the club's recent history is with the present. There are little echoes of the past, and hints at the future, everywhere.

I've looked back at the previous occasions when Watford reached the top flight to tell the stories of how those campaigns have turned out – and to see if there are any lessons to be learned. There's a forensic examination of arguably the most dramatic moment Vicarage Road has ever witnessed. I've sought to explain why I have an obsession with seeing Watford play in Europe – even the Europa League preliminary round would do – and I've met three former strikers who, although their time at Vicarage Road overlapped, have very different stories to tell. John McClelland, one of the finest centre-halves ever to pull on a yellow shirt, explains the art of defending, and I look back at the only time Watford have faced Barcelona.

That's what's in store, so all that remains is to thank a few people who have helped along the way, particularly Simon Scarsbrook, whose illustration graces the front cover, Ellis Bacon, Sam Suresh and Adam Leventhal.

I hope you enjoy the book, and I look forward to putting together further volumes of *Tales from the Vicarage* in future.

Lionel Birnie

1

When the Pozzo family took over the club in 2012, they made no secret of their aim. They wanted to reach the Premier League as soon as possible.

A near-miss at Wembley and a season spent regrouping and re-evaluating should have left the club in the perfect position to kick on.

But this is Watford, and we should know by now that things are rarely simple or straightforward. They went through three managers before settling on Slavisa Jokanovic, who fashioned a promotion-winning side where others had failed.

The title bid may have fallen short but it was nevertheless an exhilarating ride.

THE TITLE RACE

Saturday, April 18, 2015

It was almost five o'clock as Watford's supporters streamed away from Vicarage Road, satisfied that their team had done enough to move back into the Championship's automatic promotion places with just two games remaining. Victory over Birmingham City had been far from comprehensive but Craig Cathcart's flying volley was worthy of three points all on its own.

As Vicarage Road emptied, they were still playing at Dean Court. As far as we knew, Bournemouth were 2-1 up against Sheffield Wednesday, which would be enough to put the Cherries top of the table.

Suddenly, there was a cheer from the Hornet Shop, where fans had seen on television that Sheffield Wednesday had been given a penalty. Then came another, louder, cheer, which confirmed that the penalty had been scored. Outside the shop, hands reached into pockets for phones to double-check the news.

And then came a chant, which spread through the crowd dispersing from the ground: 'We. Are. Top-of-the-league. Say, we-are-top-of-the-league.'

Who'd have thought it, eh? Good old Sheffield Wednesday, scoring a late, late goal to do us a favour. I've always had a soft spot for the Owls.

Saturday, April 25, 2015

Watford had done their bit at lunchtime, winning 2-0 at Brighton and Hove Albion, which was the equivalent of laying down a strong hand in game of poker and saying to the others: 'Go on, beat that.'

The second goal, from Matej Vydra in the last minute, certainly felt decisive at the time but still Watford's fate rested on results from elsewhere later that afternoon. Whether you were in a pub near the seaside or watching the updates from the other games on television at home, that Saturday afternoon was as tense as any spent actually watching the Hornets.

The situation was clear. If Norwich City failed to win at Rotherham United and Middlesbrough lost at Fulham, Watford would be promoted. Proceed directly to the Premier League, do not pass via the play-offs, collect ninety-nine million pounds, or whatever the sum of money is these days.

At half-time, Watford had one foot in the Premier League. Norwich were drawing 0-0 and were down to ten men, while Middlesbrough trailed Fulham 1-0.

The footballing Gods toyed with Watford's fate for the rest of the afternoon as events in South Yorkshire and on the banks of the Thames swung one way, then the other. Norwich took the lead at Rotherham, which seemed to make it inevitable that Watford's bid for promotion would go to the last game. Meanwhile, Fulham stretched into a 3-1 lead, which would at least knock Middlesbrough out of the race.

The old cliché is that a season in the Football League is like a marathon, not a sprint, but that's not really true, either. The Championship is more like an egg-and-spoon race held on an obstacle course. It's not necessarily important to be at the front of the race as long as the egg is still balancing on the spoon. The aim is to just keep going, no matter what hits you. Points are never awarded for style, either. It's emotionally-draining too. From one week to the next it can be dramatic and farcical, breathtaking and mundane, exhilarating and tedious.

By 4.48pm, Middlesbrough had dragged themselves level at Craven Cottage. They'd still need snookers on the final day to catch Watford, so they went all out to win it.

Meanwhile, with four minutes remaining at Rotherham, Jordan Bowery equalised for the home side to end Norwich's hopes of catching Watford.

The pendulum swung decisively in Watford's favour when Middlesbrough, seeking a winning goal, pressed the self-destruct button. Goalkeeper Dimitrios Konstantopoulos pushed up into the Fulham penalty area when the visitors won a corner but the ball was cleared and the Greek goalkeeper lost a desperate race back into his own half as Fulham broke and Luke McCormack stroked the ball into the net.

Defeat for Middlesbrough in West London and a draw for Norwich City at Rotherham meant celebrations for Hornets everywhere, from Brighton beach to Watford town centre. The players were on the team coach, which was just arriving back at the training ground in London Colney, when they heard the news. Miguel Layun Tweeted a video of the players celebrating to his million followers.

'We. Are. Premier League, say we are Premier League.'

Saturday, May 2, 2015

Two days after Watford had confirmed their own promotion to the Premier League, Bournemouth brushed Bolton aside to join them in the top flight. But the ultimate prize – the trophy – was still in the balance. A draw or a Bolton win would have given Watford the title but Bournemouth's victory meant the destiny of the silverware would be decided on the final day of the season. Victory would clinch the biggest honour in the club's history. Watford's previous best position in the division now known as the Championship was second, in 1982. That was when they finished runners-up, eight points behind Luton Town The most significant pots in the club's trophy cabinet were the ones awarded for winning the division below this in 1969 and 1998.

There was a strange atmosphere at Vicarage Road. Lunch-time kick-offs are always slightly surreal but there was more to it than that. The most important goal had been achieved and yet there was still more to do. Watford had reached the Premier League and so there was plenty of cause for celebration but there was also a chance to make history.

Victory for Watford would clinch the Championship trophy regardless of Bournemouth's result at Charlton Athletic and so, although the Cherries scored twice in the first 12 minutes, it altered little, even if the chants from the Sheffield Wednesday fans at Vicarage Road grated. 'AFC Bournemouth are top of the league.'

Troy Deeney was denied a penalty after nine minutes but Vydra scored after 25 minutes to put Watford in charge. They could, and perhaps should, have scored again before the break to put the result beyond doubt. But, in the second half, Watford slowly ran out of steam. The second goal never came and, at times, they were clinging on.

The atmosphere was tense because the celebrations were, rightly, on hold. Promotion without having to go through the play-offs was wonderful but a piece of silverware was on offer.

With six minutes or so to go, a Mexican wave started. That's never a good sign. Some fans were eager to reproduce the adrenaline-fuelled rush onto the pitch at the end of the dramatic play-off semi-final against Leicester, and so they spilled down to the front of the Rookery end, climbed over the wall and crowded around the pitch, ready to sprint on as soon as the referee blew his whistle.

Into injury time, close enough to reach out and touch the trophy. Most of the supporters did not know it but the trophy, a podium and a big arch with the words 'Sky Bet Championship' and 'Champions' on it were all waiting in the wings to be pushed onto the pitch.

Watford conceded a free-kick too close to their own penalty area for comfort. Someone ran onto the pitch at the Vicarage Road end, kissed the goalkeeper Heurelho Gomes on the head, and had to be wrestled into the arms of the stewards by Deeney and Odion Ighalo. After such a distraction it was with crushing inevitability that the ball would bounce around in the penalty area without being properly cleared before breaking to a figure in blue and white to smash it into the net.

Imagine the cheers in the away end at The Valley when the Bournemouth fans heard. Imagine them, not trusting the cheers, reaching for their phones to see the news with their own eyes. No, on second thoughts, don't. That should have been us.

There were still a few minutes to go but the goal had been a blow to the solar plexus. Watford forced a corner or two but the way the fans crowded the edge of the pitch made it difficult for Daniel Toszer to take the kick properly.

Suddenly the impending pitch invasion seemed a bit absurd. There was a jumble of emotions and it was difficult to know which one should take priority. There was the joy of promotion, of course, but there was also frustration that the big prize had slipped away. For some supporters, it was like taking delivery of a gleaming new car only to notice a scratch on the bodywork. The trophy had been there for the taking – yellow and black ribbons ready to be tied around its elegant handles.

Bloody Sheffield Wednesday, eh…? Scoring so late to spoil our party.

* * *

Did it really matter that the trophy was snatched from our grasp at the death? If someone had told you at the start of the season that promotion would be confirmed before the last day but that the title would elude us, you'd have taken that. Let's not lose sight of the bigger picture. For only the fourth time in the club's history Watford had reached the top flight, and this was the first time since the introduction of the play-offs that they'd managed to do so automatically.

And let's face it, the summer of 2014 was one of uncertainty rather than excitement and lofty expectations. After the thrilling ride on the Zolacoaster, the train came off its rails and the Pozzo strategy began to feel like another sort of fairground attraction – one in which a blindfolded contestant threw darts at a board hoping to win a prize.

Beppe Sannino, with his broken English and his authoritarian image, which rarely extended beyond saying, 'I gaffer,' and stomping up and down on the touchline when his team was out of possession, did not really convince that he was the man to take Watford to the Premier League. He simply steadied a ship that had sprung a leak in Zola's final days, after the second wave of Pozzo signings that had contained more misses than hits. The mostly majestic libero Gabriel Angella was the exception but the likes of Javier Acuña, Essaïd Belkalem, Diego Fabbrini, Marco Faraoni and Iriney offered little improvement to the existing squad. Even Lewis McGugan, a rare English addition flattered to deceive. The reaction among Nottingham Forest supporters had been worryingly mixed. Some were sad to see McGugan leave, others volunteered to drive him down to Vicarage Road and help him hold the pen to make sure he signed on the dotted line.

Sannino had ended his first half-season with four consecutive defeats, including a 4-1 thrashing at home to Huddersfield, and risked an already unsteady relationship with his players by insisting they trained for an extra week-and-a-half after the season ended before going on their summer break.

The Pozzos' third summer saw another batch of arrivals. Heurelho Gomes, Lloyd Dyer, Keith Andrews, Gianni Munari, Juan Carlos Paredes, Craig Cathcart and Gabriel Tamas, plus the return of Matej Vydra, who'd fulfilled bench-warming duties at the Hawthorns in the interim period. It was the usual mixed bag. The Brazilian Gomes had last been seen as Tottenham's Carling Cup and Europa League goalkeeper before going on loan to Hoffenheim in Germany. Any fears that a 33-year-old goalkeeper with fewer than a dozen first-team appearances in the previous three years might be a bit rusty were soon put to bed with a string of assured performances. Dyer and Andrews seemed to have been signed to quell the criticism that the Hornets needed a few players who 'knew the division'. Dyer made himself immediately unpopular with some supporters after coming on as a substitute at Rotherham, scoring the opening goal and then running towards the bench giving the gaffer a mouthful as he went. Whatever the truth about dressing room relations, it seemed extraordinary that a player who'd only been around five minutes could be that unhappy so soon.

Andrews looked neat and tidy but too often took the sting out of an already ponderous playing style. Tamas came with a reputation as an enforcer but looked no more mobile than his predecessor Belkalem and lasted even less time, rupturing his knee ligaments against Bournemouth in September, which was the last we saw of him. Paredes looked good going forward but shaky in defence. It's impossible to say that the squad looked complete and ready for a serious tilt at automatic promotion but they did get off to a very fast start.

Bolton were thrashed 3-0 on the opening day only for a

defeat by the same score at Norwich a week later to puncture the early optimism, although there were mitigating circumstances – Joel Ekstrand was sent off after two minutes. After that, Watford won three in a row and were sitting second in the table after five league games, which makes it all the more remarkable that the 4-2 win over Huddersfield marked the end of Sannino. He resigned the following day, just as the season reached its first international break, saying he had taken the team as far as he felt he could. 'I took over a very talented squad when I arrived – but they were boys in many ways,' he said. 'I have no doubt that the squad now – who look very much like men who know exactly what they must do – are very capable of getting promotion.'

Beppe was not the man to steer the ship to the promised land but he steadied it when it was rocking and letting in water.

AUGUST

Sat 9	Bolton Wanderers	H	3-0 W	
Tue 12	Stevenage	A	1-0 W	LC
Sat 16	Norwich City	A	0-3 L	
Tue 19	Rotherham United	A	2-0 W	
Sat 23	Leeds United	H	4-1 W	
Tue 26	Doncaster Rovers	H	1-2 L	LC
Sat 30	Huddersfield Town	H	4-2 W	

League table after August 30

	P	W	D	L	F	A	Pts
1. Nottm Forest	5	4	1	0	11	3	13
2. Watford	5	4	0	1	13	6	12
3. Wolves	5	4	0	1	6	2	12
4. Norwich City	5	3	1	1	8	3	10
5. Millwall	5	3	1	1	6	3	10
6. Charlton Athletic	5	2	3	0	9	7	9

* * *

Conventional wisdom says that stability is the key to success but actually many successful environments, particularly professional sports teams, exist in a permanent state of flex and tension because stability can lead to complacency. Some people are frightened of change but others thrive when forced to stand on shifting sand. It keeps them on their toes and alert. And it must be said that it is far more important that everyone shares the same objective than it is for them all to get along famously.

If you were to write a blueprint for how to build a successful football club, you would not suggest a high turn-over of management staff. Of course, the Pozzo model has been misunderstood by plenty of observers who seem to want to portray Watford's approach as everything that is wrong with English football. But on the other hand, it was not unreasonable of some outsiders to suggest that losing the head coach while sitting second in the embryonic league table hinted at some deep malaise at Vicarage Road.

Whether Sannino's man-management style suited all the players or not, early results suggested it had not held them back. Nevertheless, speculation was rife that Sannino had jumped before he was pushed and that Watford had already lined up a replacement – a view which was not eased much by the rapid appointment of Brighton boss Oscar Garcia.

Three minutes into Garcia's first game, against Charlton Athletic at The Valley, Heurelho Gomes conceded a penalty, which Charlton scored. Watford lost the game and, 24 hours later, Garcia was admitted to hospital with chest pains. While it was tempting to joke that watching Watford can have that effect on anyone, it soon became clear that Garcia was not going to be able to take up the reins. He was still in hospital when the Hornets won 1-0 at Blackpool a week later and also missed the 1-1 draw at home to Bournemouth, when Craig Cathcart rescued a point with a late goal. Garcia's assistants Ruben Martinez and Javier Pereira and the Scot Billy McKinlay took charge of the team during Garcia's absence. McKinlay, a former Dundee United, Blackburn and Leicester player, had stepped down as Northern Ireland's assistant manager to take up a role in Garcia's coaching set-up.

On September 27, Watford went to Ewood Park and took a 2-0 first-half lead over Blackburn only to let it slip. Garcia was in the directors' box watching the game but two days later – 27 days after being appointed – it was confirmed the Spaniard had stepped down and McKinlay was promoted in his place.

That began the shortest reign of any Watford manager (or head coach) in the club's history. The highlights of a 2-1 win over Brentford were Odion Ighalo's first goal for the club and a scorching strike from Matej Vydra. At the weekend, they were held 1-1 at home by Brighton, although that result left them riding high in the table going into the second international break of the season.

On October 7, it was announced that McKinlay was leaving, after eight days, with a win and a draw as head coach – the first unbeaten manager in Watford's history. By now, the critics were having a field day, wedded to the idea that Watford was being run remotely by people who had little idea how the English Championship worked.

The situation was more complicated than that. Although McKinlay has not spoken about his brief spell in charge, or the manner of his departure, yet, it appears that the Pozzos' mother ship had been uncertain about his appointment in the first place. Clearly they favoured Slaviša Jokanovic, a Serbian who had spent a couple of years as a player at Chelsea, and had coached – without a great deal of distinction, it must be said – at Levski Sofia in Bulgaria and Hercules in Spain. He had, however, won the double in Serbia with Partizan and the Thai championship with Muanthong United.

Perhaps McKinlay was appointed in haste but, having been given the top job, he was understandably reluctant to step back down to an assistant's role for the new man, and so he was gone and Watford were onto their fourth head coach in six weeks.

In a statement, Gino Pozzo said: 'Our job is always to act in the best long-term interests of the football club. There can be no compromise on this – whatever the circumstances. I fully support and endorse the view from our technical staff that, given the talented squad which has been assembled and our position in the league, an experienced head coach with a winning pedigree is of primary importance to help ensure the success we are all striving for. The supporters of Watford have always been very understanding towards our project here and I am certain they will continue to do everything they can to support the new coach and his squad.'

What was becoming clear was that the definition of the role of manager had been completely altered. Gone – for the duration of the Italians' ownership, at least – is the idea of the old-fashioned football manager. That is a trend that many of England's top clubs have followed in recent years. The thought of one man holding the sort of power Graham Taylor enjoyed, particularly during his first spell as Watford manager, seems impossible now. How many owners will allow the fate of their investment to rest in the hands of one individual? Who will trust a manager to buy and sell players? Why would anyone change the course of their journey at the whims and fancies of a football manager?

The stability we crave is in the overall model rather than the identity of the individuals. Players and coaches will come and go, sometimes with bewildering frequency, but the overall model will remain the same. The head coach's job will be to coax the best he can out of the squad at his disposal. His input will be noted but perhaps not decisive, and when a better option presents itself the coach will be moved aside. But the ship will keep sailing in the same direction.

SEPTEMBER

Sat 13	Charlton Athletic	A	0-1 L	4th
Tue 16	Blackpool	A	1-0 W	2nd
Sat 20	Bournemouth	H	1-1 D	4th
Sat 27	Blackburn Rovers	A	2-2 D	3rd
Tue 30	Brentford	H	2-1 W	3rd

League table after September 30

	P	W	D	L	F	A	Pts
1. Norwich City	10	6	2	2	20	9	20
2. Nottm Forest	10	5	5	0	17	7	20
3. Watford	10	6	2	2	19	11	20
4. Derby County	10	5	4	1	19	10	19
5. Ipswich Town	10	5	3	2	14	8	18
6. Wolves	9	5	3	1	11	6	18

First impressions of Slaviša Jokanovic were of a brooding intensity. The smart suit paired with a beard, which looked more like it was born out of a desire not to shave every morning than anything else, said shabby chic. The tired, almost haunted eyes, hinted that a well of darkness lay behind them. Was this a man to inspire, or frighten the troops?

The early signs were good. A thumping 3-0 win at Hillsborough against Sheffield Wednesday was followed by a creditable draw against the early season high-flyers Nottingham Forest. In hindsight, that 2-2 was less impressive because it marked the start of a dramatic and irreversible slump for Stuart Pearce's men, but at the time it was a solid point, as was the draw at

Middlesbrough. We still knew very little about Jokanovic but results were good enough not to cause any immediate concern.

On November 1, Watford's closest home game to Remembrance Day, Vicarage Road marked the 100th anniversary of the start of the Great War in spectacular style. Inspired by the shirts worn by the club in 1914, the team took to the pitch in black and white stripes.

Masterminded by The 1881 Club, the supporters' group that had taken it upon itself to generate more of an atmosphere at games, the Rookery end was transformed into a sight that caused the rest of the stadium to almost skip a breath in awe. The display held aloft by the fans in the Rookery was of black and white stripes with a huge red poppy taking centre stage. It was not only a fitting tribute to the fallen but a demonstration of what can be achieved with a vision, passion and energy, and it marked a significant moment for The 1881 Club, which had been allocated a corner of the Rookery in order to better generate noise. The banners and flags that began to appear, and which celebrated the club's heritage as well as its present, were redolent of the Bundesliga, where supporters feel more a part of their clubs than mere customers. The importance of the bond between the supporters and the team is something that the club has not always appreciated but of late the connection has been re-established and, as the season wore on, it felt like the motto at the training ground in London Colney, and on one of the banners in the Rookery End – Our Time Is Now – was shared by players and fans alike.

That early November afternoon, the monochromatic Hornets did their bit by beating Millwall 3-1 to go top of the Championship. It was very tight at the summit and half a dozen other clubs could be similarly pleased with the opening third of their campaign but Watford had barely put a foot wrong so far, despite the supposed turmoil behind the scenes.

OCTOBER

Sat 4	Brighton	H	1-1 D	2nd
Sat 18	Sheffield Wednesday	A	3-0 W	1st
Tue 21	Nottingham Forest	H	2-2 D	2nd
Sat 25	Middlesbrough	A	1-1 D	2nd

League table after October 25

	P	W	D	L	F	A	Pts
1. Derby County	14	7	5	2	24	12	26
2. Watford	14	7	5	2	26	15	26
3. Wolves	14	7	5	2	21	15	26
4. Bournemouth	14	7	3	4	28	14	24
5. Middlesbrough	14	7	3	4	19	12	24
6. Norwich City	14	6	5	3	22	12	23

When accepting his player of the season award at the end-of-season dinner at Shendish Manor, Troy Deeney made a telling comment. He admitted, in front of Jokanovic, Gino Pozzo and all the assembled guests, that he and the new head coach had not hit it off at the start. He went as far to say that he wondered how long the latest man would last. 'It's fair to say we tested each other isn't it, gaffer?' Deeney said, looking across at Jokanovic's table. 'We butted heads a bit, and you realised I was the main man and I realised you were the main man.'

Having hit the top of the table, Watford then stalled. They lost 2-1 at Birmingham, having conceded very early and very late, then they lost at Ipswich before being beaten by Derby County, who looked like they were going to be the team to beat in the Championship at the time.

At the end of November, they lost 1-0 to Cardiff City to make it four defeats in a row. It was all rather reminiscent of the mini collapse exactly 12 months earlier, which culminated in a 3-0 home defeat to Yeovil and did for Gianfranco Zola.

The Cardiff game should have been a celebration of all things Watford because it was the day the club officially re-named the Rous Stand after the greatest manager in its history, Graham Taylor. It doesn't take a great deal of imagination to guess what Taylor must have made of the team's insipid performance that afternoon.

When Watford's passing game failed to ignite, they could look awfully static. A whole half could slip by without a shot or header on target. Against Cardiff they looked bright early on but, after falling behind in the 12th minute, the rest of the game was a non-event.

Four defeats in a row had seen the team tumble from the top to seventh place, two points outside the play-off zone. As ludicrous as it sounds, suddenly Jokanovic's future seemed in jeopardy. He needed to stop the rot immediately and get the promotion push back on track. November was Woe-vember.

NOVEMBER

Sat 1	Millwall	H	3-1 W	1st
Tue 4	Birmingham City	A	1-2 L	3rd
Sat 8	Ipswich Town	A	0-1 L	5th
Sat 22	Derby County	H	1-2 L	7th
Sat 29	Cardiff City	H	0-1 L	7th

League table after November 29

	P	W	D	L	F	A	Pts
1. Derby County	19	10	5	4	35	19	35
2. Ipswich Town	19	9	7	3	28	19	34
3. Brentford	19	10	4	5	30	24	34
4. Bournemouth	19	9	6	4	37	20	33
5. Middlesbrough	19	9	6	4	28	14	33
6. Blackburn Rovers	19	8	7	4	30	26	31
7. Watford	19	8	5	6	31	22	29

* * *

Every season has games that it's possible to look back at and identify as an important turning point. The 5-0 Friday-night win at Craven Cottage felt significant at the time, not just because it stopped the rot but because the Hornets were back to their free-flowing best again. It was perhaps not a coincidence that the fluidity to their play returned just as Almen Abdi got back to his best after six weeks' absence. Abdi opened the scoring with a sublime free-kick and then the Hornets were given a helping hand when Fulham goalkeeper Marcus Bettinelli was sent off for fouling Vydra in the area. Deeney scored the penalty – the first of three for him that night. But it was Abdi's second goal, Watford's fourth, that really caught the eye. One touch, a little half-turn and shimmy to open up some space and a beautiful curling shot from outside the penalty area with virtually no backlift was enough to win the goal of the season award.

Of all the players to have arrived at Vicarage Road in the past three years, the Kosovo-born Swiss international has been the most consistently enjoyable to watch. The little midfielder's technical brilliance, his eye for a pass and ability to shoot from distance set him apart from his more workmanlike colleagues and if there is a trend over the past three years, it is that Watford function far more effectively with him than without him. Only persistent and niggling injuries have prevented him from being the man around which the entire team has been constructed. In fact, Watford's stuttering campaign in 2013-14 was as much to do with Abdi's two long-term injuries as anything. His return to form just before Christmas and another run in the team in the spring helped the team step up that all important half a notch.

The Fulham result revived confidence and there was another celebratory atmosphere at Vicarage Road for the visit of Wigan Athletic in mid-December. The club had kept under wraps its plans to name the new stand on the east side of the ground after the architect of the greatest ever era, Sir Elton John, partly, one suspects, to avoid overshadowing the renaming of the Rous Stand after Graham Taylor.

But there was something entirely appropriate about the Pozzos naming opposing stands after the two men who helped power the club from the Fourth Division into the top flight in the late 1970s and 1980s. Almost all of the club's greatest days had been engineered by Taylor and Elton. The rock star's money undoubtedly helped speed the passage from the lower divisions to European competition and the FA Cup final but it was the way they embarked on their vision, ignoring all external detractors and sticking to their beliefs, that means those achievements have stood the test of time. There's an irony too in the fact that Elton paid more than £3million to build the stand opposite the one that now bears his name.

If any doubts remained about the Pozzos, these two significant gestures surely erased them. They could quite easily have sold the naming rights to the Rous Stand and the new east stand to commercial sponsors but they chose instead to honour two of the most significant people in the club's past. By recognising that past, they acknowledged that their contribution – however important it turns out to be – will be only a part of the club's rich and varied history. Elton, the local lad who watched the team from the terraces in the 1950s and 1960s and bought the club when he made his fortune in music – something that every fan dreams of doing if they were rich enough.

As *Your Song* faded, Sir Elton emerged from the tunnel with a long yellow, red and black scarf around his neck, with his partner David Furnish and young sons Zachary and Elijah, both wearing Watford hats and Harry the Hornet scarves. 'This is one of the greatest days of my life,' he said, addressing the crowd. 'I never thought I'd have a stand named after me. My years at my club were so magnificent... Watford is embedded in my heart.'

The new stand had been used a few times before but this was the first time it was close to full and, after a long wait and several false dawns, Vicarage Road was a four-side stadium to be proud of once again. While the team's performance that afternoon was not vintage stuff, they did just about enough to win 2-1 against Malky Mackay's Wigan.

Only a flat Boxing Day display against Wolves at Vicarage Road prevented the Hornets from collecting all 15 points from December and a rousing 4-2 win at Cardiff City, with two goals from Adlene Guedioura, who was completing his first loan spell from Crystal Palace, meant they ended the year back in the top five. By now Jokanovic was beating the drum for consistency. He didn't need to be an expert on the Championship to know that the turn of the year would be all-important.

DECEMBER

Fri 5	Fulham	A	5-0 W	6th
Sat 13	Wigan Athletic	H	2-1 W	6th
Sat 20	Reading	A	1-0 W	6th
Fri 26	Wolves	H	0-1 L	6th
Sun 28	Cardiff City	A	4-2 W	5th

League table after December 30

	P	W	D	L	F	A	Pts
1. Bournemouth	24	14	6	4	54	25	48
2. Ipswich Town	24	13	8	3	41	22	47
3. Derby County	24	13	6	5	46	23	45
4. Middlesbrough	24	12	7	5	38	17	43
5. Watford	24	12	5	7	43	26	41
6. Brentford	24	12	4	8	40	35	40

* * *

January heralded the now routine FA Cup third (or fourth) round tie against one of the Premier League giants. After trips to the Etihad to face Manchester City in successive seasons, the 3-0 defeat at Chelsea felt like a day to absorb and move on from without too much soul-searching, although the following weekend's 3-1 defeat at Huddersfield Town suggested it had jolted the Hornets a bit. The score was 1-0 to the Terriers when Heurelho Gomes went off injured and although Ighalo grabbed an equaliser, the home side added two in quick succession near the end. 'We did not deserve anything from the game. We only played for about ten minutes, and you have to play for the whole game,' was Jokanovic's typically blunt assessment.

Ighalo's goal may not have earned any points in Yorkshire but it did kick-start one of the most extraordinary scoring sequences in the club's history. The Nigerian striker had not looked the most refined during his early games but he had an air of unpredictability that unsettled defences and a knack of getting into the right place at the right time. He scored an incredible 14 goals in a ten-game run, including two in a 5-0 win over Charlton and four as Watford came from 2-0 down at half-time against a hopeless Blackpool side to win 7-2. That game marked a record, too, because it was the first time Watford had ever scored seven goals in a single half.

If the groans and grumbles at the interval of the game against Blackpool – who were rock-bottom and had not won away all season – were loud and clear, the second half response was emphatic. When they clicked into gear, Watford played with panache with an almost carefree commitment to attacking football. With Deeney, Vydra and now Ighalo all finding the net, opposition defences had to worry about this trident of danger. Stop Vydra's runs and Deeney would bulldoze his way through. Block Deeney and Ighalo would be there in space to bundle the ball home.

A few days after the win over Charlton it was announced that Ken Furphy had passed away at the age of 83. Furphy had been the first Watford manager to lead the club out of the lower divisions and as a result his place in history deserves to be seen as just as important as the later achievements by Graham Taylor. At the time, Watford was just another small-town club with little hope of ever making it to the top. In the 1950s and for almost all of the 1960s, the Second Division (or Championship as it is now) was little more than a mirage on the horizon. It seemed so distant to Watford that it may as well have been Narnia or Neverland. But Furphy crafted a team that was able to win the Third Division title in 1969. For two successive years he kept them in the Second Division and they reached the FA Cup semi-final, losing 5-1 to Chelsea in 1970. But for that brief flirtation with the Second Division, Elton John might never have considered putting his money into the club in the 1970s.

Furphy's passing was marked with a minute's applause before the game against Blackpool and the seven-goal comeback in the second half was more than an appropriate send-off for a man who could be said to have raised the bar for the modern-day Watford.

Just as Watford appeared to have forced their way back into contention, a referee did his best to derail them. Just 28 seconds into the game at Bournemouth, Lee Probert sent off Gabriele Angella for a clumsy, ugly lunge on Callum Wilson. Replays showed that Angella had not been the last man and a subsequent appeal saw the red card overturned – not that it made any difference because the points were already lost. To make matters worse, Bournemouth were given a penalty just before half-time and the game had to be filed among those headed,

'Just not our day.' With 18 games to play, there was still plenty of time to mount a challenge but the automatic places felt a long way off. Seven points separated Watford from the top two and it was beginning to feel like the play-offs might be the most realistic route to the Premier League.

JANUARY

Sun 4	*Chelsea*	*A*	*0-3 L*	*FA*
Sat 10	Huddersfield Town	A	1-3 L	6th
Sat 17	Charlton Athletic	H	5-0 W	6th
Sat 24	Blackpool	H	7-2 W	6th
Fri 30	Bournemouth	A	0-2 L	6th

League table after January 31

	P	W	D	L	F	A	Pts
1. Bournemouth	28	16	6	6	59	28	54
2. Derby County	28	16	6	6	52	25	54
3. Middlesbrough	28	15	8	5	43	18	53
4. Ipswich Town	28	14	9	5	46	27	41
5. Brentford	28	15	4	9	44	37	49
6. Watford	28	14	5	9	56	33	47

Now was the time to make a move, to hit upon the consistency Jokanovic craved and to keep gathering points. A late Ighalo goal was just about enough to see off Blackburn Rovers, although Gomes made an equally vital contribution with a stunning save before that.

This was the phase of the season where the motto must be, 'Never mind the quality, count the points.' That was certainly the case at Griffin Park – venue for an old-school, last-minute terrace bundle on a night that felt like the pendulum was swinging Watford's way.

Okay, so it wasn't quite as momentous as the victory at Port

Vale during the 1999 run-in, but it was one of those games where Watford seemed to contrive to do everything they could to lose yet came away with three points.

Brentford were reduced to ten men in the first half, yet took the lead early in the second. A few minutes later, Watford had a great chance to claw themselves level when they were awarded a penalty after a handball in the box, but Deeney's weak penalty was saved low down by the Bees keeper. After that, the Hornets scrapped hard and Ighalo popped up to head an equaliser but the winner seemed destined to evade them.

That was until injury time when Vydra slid the ball across the box and Ighalo instinctively swung a boot at it to spark delirious scenes behind the goal.

If that was a case of getting out of jail, the following Saturday's trip to Bolton Wanderers was like escaping from Alcatraz and swimming across the bay to have a coffee in San Francisco. In a good old-fashioned see-saw of a contest, Watford swung from 1-0 up to 2-1 down at half-time. They came out fighting in the second half and got themselves 3-2 ahead only for Bolton to equalise with five minutes remaining. Two points seemed to have slipped away but Deeney popped up in the box to secure a brilliant 4-3 win.

Of course, just as Watford got up to sprinting pace they clattered into a hurdle. The 3-0 defeat at home to Norwich City was alarming not just because of the meek way Watford surrendered in the final third of the game but the fact that the Canaries had overtaken them in the table. By now the race for the title, the other automatic promotion place and the spots in the play-offs were one big free-for-all, open to as many as eight teams. While the neutrals got worked up into a lather about how tight it was at the top, those of us involved in the scramble for places were beginning to feel the heat. With so many games still to go, it seemed madness to increase the pressure and study the fixtures and work out who might drop points where, and yet many of us did.

Convincing back-to-back wins over Rotherham and Leeds lifted Watford up to third place in the table, just on the shoulders of Derby and Middlesbrough, who seemed to have established themselves as favourites to go up. That just shows how unpredictable the Championship is because at the end of the season neither of them were promoted.

FEBRUARY

Sat 7	Blackburn Rovers	H	1-0 W	6th
Tue 10	Brentford	A	2-1 W	5th
Sat 14	Bolton Wanderers	A	4-3 W	5th
Sat 21	Norwich City	H	0-3 L	6th
Tue 24	Rotherham United	H	3-0 W	6th
Sat 28	Leeds United	A	3-2 W	3rd

League table after February 28

	P	W	D	L	F	A	Pts
1. Derby County	34	19	8	7	66	35	65
2. Middlesbrough	34	18	9	7	50	24	63
3. Watford	34	19	5	10	69	42	62
4. Bournemouth	34	17	9	8	67	37	60
5. Ipswich Town	33	17	9	7	54	34	60
6. Norwich City	33	17	8	8	64	37	59

The 2-2 draw at Wolves was overshadowed by the news that a 44-year-old Watford supporter called Nic Cruwys had been attacked after the game and left in a critical condition. The following Saturday, as Watford took on Reading, and led by The 1881, Vicarage Road broke into applause in the 44th minute as a gesture of support and solidarity for their fellow supporter. At the time there was no certainty that Mr Cruwys would pull through and the thought that someone could end the afternoon supporting their team in intensive care seemed to be something that had been consigned to history. Fortunately, within a few weeks, Mr Cruwys's condition improved but the shock of the attack had brought everyone connected with Watford Football Club together. The players contributed to a fund set up to help his family while Nic was in hospital, Sir Elton sent a message of support and the phrase, 'For Nic, For Promotion,' was coined.

The team did their bit too, thrashing a poor Reading side that had both eyes on their upcoming FA Cup semi-final, 4-1. That result hoisted them back into the top two. Incredibly, in the space of six weeks, and 11 games, Watford had forced their way firmly into the hunt for an automatic promotion place.

Still, though, only six points separated the top six and so the race was coming down to a test of nerves. Victory at Wigan put Watford top of the Championship for the first time since that win over Millwall back in November, albeit only on goal difference, and there was a feeling that they were timing their charge perfectly, like a good 400-metre runner hitting the front as they entered the final bend.

Again, though, they were set to stumble just as they'd got their noses in front. Mick McCarthy's dogged, determined Ipswich side came to Vicarage Road to frustrate and keep themselves in the hunt for a play-off place. The game was destined to end goalless until the fifth minute of injury time when a high ball caught out the Watford defence and left Ipswich two against one. Freddie Sears squared the ball to Richard Chaplow who slotted past Gomes to complete the smash-and-grab.

It is too painful to reflect now that had Watford's defence held firm that afternoon, they'd have been champions. Little did we know at the time that so many last-minute goals would shape the outcome of the season.

MARCH

Tue 3	Fulham	H	1-0 W	3rd
Sat 7	Wolves	A	2-2 D	3rd
Sat 14	Reading	H	4-1 W	2nd
Tue 17	Wigan Athletic	A	2-0 W	1st
Sat 21	Ipswich Town	H	0-1 L	2nd

League table after March 21

	P	W	D	L	F	A	Pts
1. Bournemouth	39	21	10	8	82	40	73
2. Watford	39	22	6	11	78	46	72
3. Middlesbrough	39	21	9	9	59	30	72
4. Norwich City	39	20	10	9	76	43	70
5. Derby County	39	19	10	10	69	43	67
6. Ipswich Town	39	19	10	10	59	43	67

On paper, Easter looked like either a chance to take control of the situation, or a potential nightmare, depending on your mood. In the run-up to the games at Derby and at home to Middlesbrough, it was possible to imagine any scenarios ranging from Watford collecting six points to them ending the weekend empty-handed. By Good Friday, Derby were buckling, without a win in six and, of the top sides, the ones who were feeling the heat most. Their fans were edgy but that did not make them easy opponents. Vydra gave Watford the lead but the odds were against them when Marco Motta was sent off for a foul in the area and Darren Bent struck the equaliser from the spot. When the Rams took the lead in the second half, Watford could have folded but they dug deep. With Ben Watson and Adlene Guedioura adding guts and guile in midfield, they were no pushovers and they finally got their reward when Ighalo pounced to equalise.

Easter Monday was another huge occasion and Watford

brushed aside a surprisingly poor Middlesbrough team. On that evidence it seemed remarkable that Boro's Patrick Bamford was eventually voted the Championship's player of the season ahead of Troy Deeney, because when it mattered most Bamford offered very little.

With five games to go, Watford were still the hunters rather than the hunted. They were in third place waiting for one of the sides ahead of them to miss a step. All they could do was keep winning, and that is what they did. Millwall were swatted aside on what could have been a potentially hazardous trip to south-east London. Suddenly every fixture looked like a banana skin. Nottingham Forest had nothing to play for apart from pride but a midweek trip to the City Ground is never a picnic.

And, as Watford's three main rivals had all won the previous evening, the pressure was on.

Ighalo's fourth-minute header was straight out of the Graham Taylor play-book. A near-post corner was flicked on by Craig Cathcart and Ighalo was waiting at the far post to force it home. Just before half-time Matthew Connolly, a local lad who was on loan from Cardiff City and who added a welcome bit of steel to the defence, strolled forward with the ball like Franz Beckenbauer. He kept going forward and stayed up in the Forest area so that when the ball broke to him, he was ready to lash it home. Forest had a man sent off in the second half, then pulled a goal back and, for 15 minutes or so, it was all very edgy until Abdi put the result beyond doubt late on.

The remarkable thing was that, despite suffering only one defeat in 11 games, Watford were still only third. Bournemouth were top, a point ahead of Norwich, who had slightly superior goal difference. Craig Cathcart's goal and Bournemouth's slip-up against Sheffield Wednesday finally put Watford top of the table with two games remaining. Now all they had to do was hold it together and a place in the Premier League was theirs.

APRIL

Fri 3	Derby County	A	2-2 D	4th
Mon 6	Middlesbrough	H	2-0 W	3rd
Sat 11	Millwall	A	2-0 W	3rd
Wed 15	Nottingham Forest	A	3-1 W	3rd
Sat 18	Birmingham City	H	1-0 W	1st
Sat 25	Brighton	A	2-0 W	1st

MAY

| Sat 2 | Sheffield Wednesday | H | 1-1 D | 2nd |

Final table

	P	W	D	L	F	A	Pts
1. Bournemouth	46	26	12	8	98	45	90
2. Watford	46	27	8	11	91	50	89
3. Norwich City	46	25	11	10	88	48	86
4. Middlesbrough	46	25	10	11	68	37	85
5. Brentford	46	23	9	14	78	59	78
6. Ipswich Town	46	22	12	12	72	54	78

The goal was always to reach the Premier League and unlock the riches that would help transform Watford's fortunes. Back in the 1980s, when they reached the top flight for the first time, there was a sense of elation at breaking new ground. Over the next six seasons, Watford established themselves as a top-ten club. The two brief visits to the Premier League since have been coloured by a slight sense of not belonging, like being the unwelcome guests at a party it's cost a fortune to attend.

Achieving automatic promotion meant Watford returned to the top flight through the front door. The bookies might still make them among the favourites for relegation but there could be no doubt that the foundations felt stronger than before.

The disappointment of missing out on the trophy and the

medals soon faded as thousands turned out to see the open-top bus parade through the town. The players and coaching staff wrote their names in the history books alongside all the others who have ever achieved anything for the club. We knew we might not see some of them again but we thanked them for their contribution. But what nobody could have known that sunny day in Cassiobury Park was that the man who had led them over the line would go no further.

Within a couple of weeks it emerged that Jokanovic and the club were well adrift as talks continued to renew the head coach's expired contract. Reports in the media varied wildly. Depending on what you read, Jokanovic was being spectacularly greedy or the club was being incredibly parsimonious. The truth most likely settles somewhere in between and it is just as likely that the club had their eyes on someone else to take the team to the next level.

Jokanovic was hired to get the club promoted. He'd done his part and it does not necessarily follow that he was the man they had in mind to establish the team in the Premier League.

Although Jokanovic will not stalk the touchline at Vicarage Road in the Premier League, the success he created will never be forgotten. The team he moulded and finessed did something that only one other Watford team in history has managed.

They came within moments of greatness too, but, in the pragmatic world of modern football the trophy would have meant little if it was to be followed by immediate relegation.

Whatever the future holds, the class of 2014-15 and their achievements will only be fully appreciated as time goes on. In the short term there was too much excitement about promotion to the Premier League and that entails, too much change, to really examine the significance of what they had done. Football defies that cliché about the enjoyment being in the journey rather than the destination but whether the club establishes itself in the top flight or not, the team that won promotion will have legendary status bestowed upon it and will go down as one of the most exciting sides ever to grace Vicarage Road.

* * *

The pages turn so quickly now. Once it was confirmed that Jokanovic would not continue as Watford's head coach, the conveyor belt whirred into life action and delivered the next man into the hot seat: Enrique Sánchez Flores, or Quique for short. As is now the custom, Watford supporters everywhere headed to the internet to glean a few facts about the new man.

A long playing career at Valencia and Real Madrid yielded a clutch of caps for Spain and after that a coaching career that has taken him to Getafe, Valencia, Benfica and Atletico Madrid. Most impressive of all was victory in the Europa League with Atletico Madrid in 2010.

Over the course of a summer, the face of the squad changed again. There would be new names to learn and faces to familiar-ise ourselves with. Recent history tells us that some will become firm favourites and others will fall by the wayside. It's a fact, too, that some of those who served with distinction during the rise will not make the grade.

But as the present continues its ceaseless pursuit of the future, so too will the achievements of the new generation's immediate predecessors solidify in our minds. In time the joy of promotion to the Premier League in 2015 will become another memory to summon up in leaner times.

The uncontrollable joy at Ighalo's winner at Griffin Park, the majesty of Abdi's finish at Craven Cottage, the gravity-defying stop by Gomes against Blackburn, Deeney running towards us, slapping his palm on his chest as he does after almost every goal...

2

Going up is one thing, staying up is another challenge altogether.

In 1982, Watford took England's elite by storm, finishing runners-up at the first attempt. The game has changed since then and the gap between the top two divisions is now a chasm.

But what lessons can be learned from the previous two short-lived stints?

Here, we look at the club's three previous promotions to the top flight and how things turned out.

GOING UP, STAYING UP?

1982-83

When Watford earned promotion to the top division for the first time in the club's history in 1982, Graham Taylor was determined to make sure his players were ready for the challenge. The manager told his squad: 'We may not be the best but there's no reason we can't be the fittest.'

Taylor took the players to Norway for a pre-season block of training that Les Taylor described in *Enjoy the Game* as 'a boot camp'. Ian Bolton added, 'It was like being in the army,' and Wilf Rostron, who rarely raised a word in protest, said: 'The manager killed us that pre-season. It was literally morning, noon and night and, oh, how we grumbled.'

The team stayed at a dormitory and each morning ran a mile or so to their training ground to do a session before running back for breakfast. After eating, it was back to the training ground for a full day's work, and every other evening they played a 90-minute match against a local team before collapsing into bed to rest and start it all over again the next morning.

Confident that his men were physically fit, Taylor was also prepared to gamble that they were skilled enough to cope, even though only a handful of them had experience of playing at the top level. Pat Rice had been part of Arsenal's 1971 double-winning side, of course, and Gerry Armstrong had just returned from the World Cup, where he had scored Northern

Ireland's winner against the hosts, Spain, but much of the rest of the squad had come up with the Hornets from the lower divisions, or had graduated from the youth team.

It is incredible to look back and realise that Taylor made only one signing that summer, as he prepared to take on the best sides in England, splashing out £15,000 on Richard Jobson from non-league Burton Albion. That perhaps emphasises how vast the gap between the top two divisions has grown in the subsequent two decades, particularly since the formation of the Premier League in 1992, but don't be fooled into thinking the top flight in 1982-83 was a soft touch. English teams had won the past six European Cups and, although there may not have been the number of foreign players there are today, the likes of Liverpool, Manchester United, Arsenal and Tottenham could cherry-pick the best players.

Having said that, the First Division then was more open and smaller clubs could dream. Nottingham Forest had won the title in 1978 just a year after gaining promotion from the Second Division; Aston Villa were champions in 1981, the year Ipswich Town came mighty close. No one was expecting Watford to trouble the top places in the table but nor were newly-promoted clubs written off and condemned to relegation before a ball was kicked. They could at least dare to dream.

Besides, Watford had already ruffled feathers by spoiling reputations and causing supposedly more sophisticated opponents to run out of breath and get mud on their shorts. They had developed a pedigree as cup giant-killers, knocking Manchester United out of the League Cup in 1978 before stunning Southampton 7-1 and slaying European champions Forest 4-1 in the same competition two years later. In January 1982, they beat Manchester United again, this time in the FA Cup, with a goal from Jan Lohman that had been worked out on the training ground. The Hornets battered United that day because they did not fear the badge on their opponents' chests. Before the game, Les Taylor banged on United's dressing room door and shouted: 'Come on then, we'll be waiting for you.' As they walked off the pitch, Ian Bolton said to United's Martin Buchan: 'See you next year.'

Knocking United out of the cup made headlines, of course, but as the Hornets closed in on promotion, Fleet Street's finest journalists headed to Vicarage Road to see what the First Division was in for. Not all of them liked what they witnessed.

They didn't see a high-tempo, attacking game that unsettled defenders because fitter and stronger forwards took them well outside their comfort zone. They didn't see the intricate movements that opened up space. They didn't see a pair of wingers who could cross the ball with incredible accuracy and, in the case of John Barnes, leave a full-back's head spinning. They didn't see two hard-working central midfielders who chased and harried and closed down their opponents, forcing them into mistakes. And they didn't appreciate the ten, 12 or 15 shots on target every match and some of the most entertaining football there was to see.

Instead, they saw a succession of long balls hit hopefully towards a big centre forward and a swarm of Hornets feeding off the scraps.

Towards the end of the season, when promotion had been confirmed, Taylor spoke to Match of the Day's John Motson as questions about Watford's style continued. Received wisdom was that Watford would have to adapt to survive in the First Division. Taylor never had a lot of time for received wisdom.

'We keep getting asked this about our style of play and I don't really know what the style of play is,' he said. 'What we do, we want to go forward and get the ball in the box as often as possible.

'If you say to me, "Will you change your approach or your

attitude to the game?" I will say emphatically, "No." As regards style, I'll leave it for all the experts to decide what style we're giving. We've been described in some quarters as simply a kick-and-rush side and I find that quite amazing that people in the game can say there's a kick-and-rush side while we're sitting second in the division, having scored 70-odd goals. If it is as simple as that then I think everybody should kick and rush it, but you know as well as I do, John, it's not as simple as that.'

Motson then suggested that the First Division may be 'more sophisticated' and that Watford might need to become more technically proficient, more patient.

'More sophisticated?' said Taylor, almost spitting the word out. 'I hate that word being used where football is concerned. Football is a simple game. It's not a sophisticated game. It's a game for the man on the terraces, it's a game to excite people. I know this: whatever level of football I watch, the man on the terrace, when he sees something that is going to be exciting, and usually it is in and around the penalty box, he will start to take great interest. He is not interested, in my opinion, in watching people play 15, 16 consecutive passes in their own half of the field. Now if we try to tell him he has to become more sophisticated, I think what he will say to us, as in fact he has been saying in the past few years is, "I won't bother coming to watch you because I just want to get excited."

'I hate sophisticated football,' Taylor added for emphasis. 'You can't crack this game. You're learning all of the time. And if we have to learn in the First Division, we'll learn all right, or we'll try our best to learn.'

* * *

When the fixtures for the 2015-16 season were published, they contained a staggering coincidence, one which would have had mathematicians trying to work out the probability of it happening. In 1982-83, Watford's first five opponents were Everton (home, won 2-0), Southampton (away, won 4-1), Manchester City (away, lost 0-1), Swansea City (home, won 2-1) and West Bromwich Albion (home, won 4-0). Thirty three years later, the fixture computer decided that Watford would face the same five opponents at the start of their latest season at the top: Everton (away), West Bromwich Albion (home), Southampton (home), Manchester City (away) and Swansea City (home).

Never mind the mathematicians, what odds would a bookmaker have given on Watford's class of 2015 earning 12 points from the first five games as their predecessors did in 1982?

To say the Hornets hit the ground running is an understatement. They stunned the complacent and rattled the cages of the establishment. World Cup hero Gerry Armstrong scored the club's first-ever top flight goal in the 2-0 win over Everton on a sunny afternoon at Vicarage Road but the Toffees were not the only team to melt in the face of Watford's white heat. A few days later at The Dell, Southampton were handed a beating every bit as shocking as the 7-1 League Cup defeat they'd suffered in 1980.

A couple of months earlier, Southampton's midfielder Alan Ball had been on the same flight to Australia as the Watford team. Watford were heading off for an end-of-season tour Down Under, Ball was going to play for an Australian side over his summer break and earn a few extra quid. On the plane, Watford's players had a few drinks with the England World Cup winner, who was winding them up about the coming season. 'Wait until you get in the First Division. We'll show you how to play football.'

After trouncing the Saints 4-1, Taylor waited for Ball to come off the pitch. 'Not bad for a side that can't fucking play, are we?' It was good-natured stuff and Ball took it well, admitting that they'd been no match for Watford and accepting that their game wasn't just about energy and enthusiasm but was pretty skilful too.

The 3-0 victory over West Bromwich Albion on September 11, 1982, put Watford top of the league for the first and only week in their history, and two weeks after that they slaughtered Sunderland, beating them 4-0 in each half after Taylor had refused to let the players sit down during the break, instead putting them through their pre-match warm-up routine again to make sure they didn't ease up on the hapless Wearsiders.

Taylor had not taken the First Division lightly. He had prepared his team meticulously, but he was true to his word and he stuck to the principles that had gained promotion in the first place. His mantra was simple: 'Get it, give it, find a fresh position.' The idea was to pass and move and keep the opposition moving too, until they were out of position and out of puff. Taylor makes no bones about it: Watford were direct, but they were not aimlessly hoofing the ball up the pitch and running after it. There was a method to the way they played and it had been devised and tweaked over the years based on a theory he'd adopted when managing at Lincoln that the more shots on goal a team had, the more chance they had of winning.

In the days before computers and the Opta statistics, long before possession of the football was expressed as a percentage – as if that means anything on its own – Taylor employed data analysts to watch Watford's games and compile incredibly detailed reports. Every pass, tackle and shot was noted, as were the positions on the pitch that they took place. In the final analysis, and in short-hand terms, a pass forwards meant something, a pass sideways or backwards did not. A shot that hit the target and forced the goalkeeper to make a save counted, one that whistled wide did not.

And Taylor prepared his team to treat Liverpool, Arsenal

and Manchester United no differently to the teams they had faced during their rise through the divisions. He intended to challenge the top sides to show just how good they were and, if Watford got a good thumping every now and then, so be it. He was confident his team would score goals, win games and surprise a few people.

One of the men who analysed games for Watford agreed with him. A firm of bookmakers offered Watford a huge points handicap for the season and the data analyst put his money on the line, turning a £500 stake into £10,000 winnings.

* * *

It wasn't until November that the backlash really began. Watford had slipped a little, down to eighth in the table – their lowest position all season – and many were anticipating a steady slide towards the bottom. But the Hornets refused to sink. Instead, they won consecutive away league games at Tottenham and Arsenal to move back up to second place. The 1-0 victory at Spurs, thanks to a late Les Taylor strike, really upset the purists because Watford refused to allow the elegant Glenn Hoddle time on the ball. At the end of the month, Arsenal were smashed 4-2 at Highbury and the newspaper columnists let rip. Watford were likened to a pack of wild dogs with all the negative connotations that went with it – snapping and snarling, wild-eyed and untamed. If some commentators were to be believed, they represented everything that was wrong with the English game.

Now, that sounds familiar.

* * *

Watford continued to win games and, although the most

eye-catching results came in the first half of the season, it was after Christmas that they consolidated and set themselves on course to qualify for European competition. Taylor accepts they were a team that either won or lost – they drew only two of their last 31 league games that season – and that they didn't keep many clean sheets. But they scored lots of goals – 74 in the league. Only Liverpool scored more. Luther Blissett, who had risen with Watford from the Fourth Division, was the top scorer, winning the golden boot, and he forced his way into the England squad.

Victory over Liverpool on the final day of the season secured their position as runners-up, which earned them a place in the Uefa Cup (the predecessor of the Europa League). In those days, only the champions qualified for the European Cup – the elite competition.

The 1982-83 season still represents the high-water mark for the club and it will remain so until Watford win the Premier League...

In a way, though, such startling first-time success set the bar unattainably high for Graham Taylor. Yes, the club reached the FA Cup final the following season, losing to Everton, but it's fair to say that the cups offered Watford the best hope of further success. The subsequent league positions achieved under Taylor were 11th, 11th, 12th and ninth – meaning an average of ninth over his six years at the helm in the First Division.

Elton John and Graham Taylor took the club from the Fourth Division and established them as one of the top ten best clubs in England. Stands named after the two men now face one another at Vicarage Road in recognition of that fact and it is somehow fitting that they are, symbolically at least, watching over an era during which Gino Pozzo and the rest hope to emulate, or at least challenge and perhaps surpass, some of those past heroics.

1999-00

The years between Graham Taylor's two spells as manager barely need to be described in detail here. If you remember them, you'll know what it was like. It felt as if the sun had dipped down below the Rous Stand, as it was called then, causing the temperature to drop and the light to fade. For ten years the club battled on in this frosty gloom.

Elton had tried to sell the club to Robert Maxwell in 1987. Fortunately, the deal was blocked by the Football League because of Maxwell's interests in Oxford United and Derby County. Three years later, Jack Petchey took the club on and, until the end at least, steered a course that skirted around oblivion. In his autobiography *50/50 Man: The Jack Petchey Story*, he devotes all of one page to his time at Vicarage Road, saying: 'Buying into Watford was not the best move I have ever made. I don't believe I was ever truly accepted by either the team, the staff, or the fans, particularly the fans – no matter what you did, you were wrong!

'Believe me, being a football chairman is not as glamorous as it sounds and I was more than happy – no, relieved – to hand back the reins to Elton John when he felt able to take the club back.'

Petchey's lack of popularity owed itself to a number of factors. For a start, he had been a West Ham director and was a Hammers fan. He'd built his fortune as a car dealer and seller of timeshare holiday apartments – nothing wrong with that – but it didn't lessen the image of an East End barrow boy made good. But the root of his problems with the supporters was that Watford was not a passion or a hobby to be indulged. He ran the club prudently and he wasn't prepared to sink more money into it than the business could justify. Really, Petchey's heart wasn't in it the way Elton's had been, and it showed.

The problem was that the early 1990s were a time of dramatic change in English football. The Hillsborough disaster in 1989 led to the Taylor Report, which meant all clubs in the top two divisions had to make their grounds all-seater. Petchey must take some credit for building the stand at the Vicarage Road end and then the Rookery, but it did not escape the fans that he sold Paul Furlong and Bruce Dyer to finance it.

After years of trying to break away from the Football League, the top clubs finally formed the Premier League in 1992. Watford's chairman and chief executive had been sitting round the table with their counterparts from Manchester United, Arsenal, Liverpool and the rest in the mid-1980s when secret talks over a 'Super League' first began but as the Premier League's teams cruised into the sunset on their luxury liner, Watford were among the clubs fighting over the lifejackets and climbing into a rowing boat.

By 1996, even Petchey recognised that if the ship sunk, his asset would plummet in value. With relegation to the third tier on the cards, he authorised the SOS call to the club's favourite son, Graham Taylor, knowing it might also persuade Elton to take the club on again.

Taylor's Second Coming was not the smoothest of resurrections. The team failed to avoid relegation, then spent a year treading water before it recovered. It took that season and a bit for all the pieces to slot into place. Elton did come back, as the figurehead of a large consortium of directors who came to Watford, and football, from other walks of life. They were greeted as the club's saviours and one or two of them enjoyed the adulation to such an extent that they were nicknamed 'the milkmen' for their habit of walking in front of applauding supporters before home games. In truth, the supporters were clapping them mostly for being Not Jack Petchey.

When Taylor took charge of the team again, he rebuilt the

team and engineered two successive promotions, taking them into the top flight, where he'd left them in 1987. It was an exhilarating rise, with more than a hint of déja-vu but, reflecting on that era now, it's clear it all happened too quickly. Most of the team that Taylor led out of the Second Division were playing in the Premiership 15 months later and it was too soon, and too much, for many of them. Even the reinforcements signed during the briefest pause for breath in the First Division were never likely to add enough.

But no one would have turned down promotion and many, those who witnessed the first Taylor era in particular, believed the manager could work miracles again.

The major problem was that Watford still owed Jack Petchey £2.5million – a sum of money that could be paid off cheaply if it was settled immediately on reaching the Premiership but which would, according to the terms of the sale, rise if they chose to pay it off in instalments.

Those expecting the club to be awash with Premiership cash were to be disappointed. Taylor would have to wait for the second chunk of money to come in later in the season because the old owner had to be repaid first.

In 1982, Taylor hit the top flight without adding significant new signings through choice. This time, he had no alternative but to go with what he had, picking up a couple of free transfers to cover the gaps.

Des Lyttle arrived from Nottingham Forest to replace the marauding Darren Bazeley, who opted to join Wolves and skip the Premiership experience. Lyttle had been a solid enough defender but he'd lost his way at Forest and had spent the previous season in the reserves and on loan at Port Vale. He was not a typical Taylor full-back, and played as though the halfway line was protected by an invisible forcefield that prevented him from crossing. The other arrival, Mark Williams, looked much more promising, initially at least. An elegant, often composed centre half with a fighter's heart and the sort of mean streak you want in defenders, he had played alongside Sean Dyche in the Chesterfield side that reached the FA Cup semi-final in 1997. But that was the extent of his experience – his career to date had all been spent in the lower divisions. Initially, he looked like he might make the step up, but the occasional rush of blood to the head became more frequent and he lost his regular place in the side in the autumn.

The first thing to note was that the gap between the top sides and the newly promoted teams had widened since 1982. In the summer of 1999, as Watford added two free-transfer signings, Arsenal signed a young French winger called Thierry Henry from Juventus for more than £10million. Chelsea signed Chris Sutton for a similar fee. Heck, even Sunderland splashed out £4m on Stefan Schwarz. Transfer fees had accelerated to the point that a couple of million quid got you someone to keep the bench warm. Watford had been left behind in this regard – the most they'd ever paid for a player was still the £550,000 it cost to bring Luther Blissett home from Milan in 1984.

Pre-season was far from ideal. Not only was it the shortest gap between the end of one season and the start of the next that Watford had ever had, but there had been little time to organise matches against suitably testing opposition. They were committed to travelling to the Isle of Man Steam Packet Festival, partly because they were reluctant to let down the organisers and partly because they were short of alternatives. Even the ever-optimistic Tommy Mooney described it as 'a crap trip... just not what we needed at all.' Watford beat an Isle of Man XI 1-0 and drew with Tranmere Rovers 1-1. Then they went to Dublin to face St Patrick's Athletic before tackling the most difficult league in the world.

* * *

The first match, at home to Wimbledon, looked winnable. This brought Taylor up against Egil Olsen, who had managed the Norway team that did for England's World Cup qualification hopes in 1993 and that, in turn, brought the media spotlight to Vicarage Road.

Alec Chamberlain, the goalkeeper, had dislocated his finger during the Isle of Man trip. Micah Hyde, Paul Robinson, Allan Smart and Nick Wright also missed the start of the season. Add Bazeley to that list and Watford were without half of their Wembley heroes.

The unforgiving nature of the Premiership was made apparent in that first game. Having twice dragged themselves back into contention, a terrible mix-up in the penalty area and a spectacular own goal from Richard Johnson gave Wimbledon a 3-2 victory. It was harsh on Johnson and the rest of the team but an early warning that even bang-average sides like Wimbledon punished mistakes ruthlessly.

Back-to-back 1-0 wins at Liverpool and against Bradford were as good as the season got. They never won two in a row again, in fact; the remaining four league victories came with a frequency that made Halley's Comet seem like a regular visitor.

From late August onwards, the campaign was a slog; a battle to keep the spirits up in the face of repeated disappointment. The 1-0 win over Chelsea in September was memorable for more than its rarity. It was a day when hard work, guts, determination and skill combined to secure the points.

At first the defeats were narrow – 1-0 against Aston Villa, Leicester, West Ham and Arsenal – and supporters could cling to the hope that things might turn. A horrendous run of fixtures, where they faced the previous season's top five all in a row, broke that resolve, despite the win over Chelsea. At the time, the 4-1 defeat against Manchester United, the holders of the treble, felt like it might signal that the worst was over. Things were supposed to get easier after that but it was as if the team reached that point, beaten, bowed but having avoided total humiliation, and expected to be able to take a breather.

The results that followed felt a whole lot worse – a 3-1 defeat at home to Middlesbrough, who were no great shakes, then a 4-0 thumping at Coventry, an undeserved defeat against Sunderland and then, the nadir: a 5-0 thrashing by Wimbledon at Selhurst Park, with each one of their goals greeted by a moronic fanfare over the public address system.

After the 4-0 defeat at Tottenham on Boxing Day, Watford had collected just two points from 11 games.

The Premiership was just too much and it was hard to have much fun as the optimism ebbed away. It was very strange for Watford supporters to sense Taylor's powerlessness because it was not something they had witnessed before, but the solution was not to be found up the manager's sleeve.

Even the new players that came in had a limited impact. Nordin Wooter, the diminutive, dreadlocked winger brilliantly likened to a small, burrowing creature by the website Blind, Stupid and Desperate, looked like a world beater on his victorious debut against Chelsea. He'd arrived from Real Zaragoza for £950,000, a club record fee, a few days before that game. There was genuine excitement at having signed someone who'd played in the 1996 Champions League final for Ajax. Wooter had pace but, to expand on that earlier comparison, he played like a super-charged mole, with vision to match. Yes, he was quick but too often he dribbled the ball into his mole hole and disappeared from view.

Xavier Gravelaine strolled on set as if he was the star of his own avant-garde film, shot in black and white, of course. He left an enigmatic twirl of cigarette smoke in his wake and his chief mode of expression was a Gallic shrug that oozed contempt. Eric Cantona got away with that sort of thing because he was capable of brilliance in many of the matches he played.

Gravelaine played only when he fancied it, and he fancied it only once – in a game against Southampton over Christmas when he scored twice in a thrilling 3-2 win.

That was the only time a smile played across his lips and the dark bags under his eyes, which looked as if they carried in them the weight of the world, lightened a little. The rest of the time he skulked in the shadows, waved his arms dismissively and then he disappeared just as quickly as he'd arrived, leaving everyone who'd come into contact with him scratching their heads and wondering whether he'd existed at all or whether he'd been a bizarre apparition.

Then there was Heidar Helguson – a bona fide superhero in the making and an epoch-defining signing who was worth every penny of the £1.5m he cost from Norwegian side Lillestrom. The Icelandic centre forward was not the quickest, nor the deadliest, nor the most technically gifted but he had enough of everything that, when combined with a Mooney-esque refusal to be beaten, he became a star.

Sadly, though, the season was over as a going concern long before the end. Membership of the Premiership, which had marketed itself as the gleaming, exclusive place to be, was not all it was cracked up to be. Cash was now the panacea, success meant spend, spend, spend. Players were not only defined by their transfer fee but by their reported weekly wage, and the sums were already mind-boggling.

The rules of the game had changed but the money generated by one season among the elite might, if spent carefully, turn Watford first into a yo-yo club and then help them gain a foothold.

2006-07

If promotion in 1999 had been unexpected, the return seven years later was improbable. This time, the road in between had not been a dreary dual carriageway to nowhere, as it had been in the 1990s, but an unlit mountain road with treacherous hairpins, off-camber corners and terrifying descents.

It could be argued that Watford's brush with the rarified air of the Premiership left some at the top of the club light-headed and dizzy. While Taylor preached the need for pragmatism, of establishing the club as one of the top 30 in the country, you could almost sense the chorus of 'boring' from some in the boardroom. Forget that; let's go for glamour and excitement. Let's send for Gianluca Vialli.

Again, there's no need to labour the point here about the wrong-headedness of that decision, but we all saw the consequences when supporters were rattling the begging buckets to save the club from administration not 18 months after the Italian's appointment. It's not fair to point all the blame at Vialli, or even the men who sanctioned his spending, just as it is not right to absolve them because of the collapse of the broadcaster ITV Digital. Losing money that had been included in the budget was like asking the driver, as he negotiated that steep mountain descent, to switch off his headlights and take his hands off the wheel and hope for the best.

Miraculously, Watford did not plunge over the edge, and the man who helped prevent a detour into oblivion, Ray Lewington, did so with good grace and the patience of a saint, agreeing to have his budget cut year after year and finally paying for it with his job. Lewington had been a safe pair of hands but many supporters grew tired of the Sunday-driver school of management. Lewington's replacement was the almost unknown Aidy Boothroyd – a journeyman defender from the lower divisions who had never managed before but had worked with Watford's chief executive, Mark Ashton, at West Brom. It's not what you know...

Boothroyd had a shaky start, with just two wins from his first seven games, but the Hornets stayed up by a couple of points. Over the summer of 2005, Boothroyd swept through the place like a whirlwind. His confidence was infectious and, after a few false starts in the transfer market, he was allowed more money than Lewington had ever been afforded to bolster the squad.

He quickly assembled the nucleus of a team – revitalising some of the existing players – and adding Ben Foster, Clark Carlisle, Malky Mackay, Matt Spring, Darius Henderson and Marlon King. By any standards, that is the spine of a very good Championship side. Add Ashley Young – the finest product of the youth system since the 1980s – and there was clearly potential to aspire to more than a relegation battle.

But it was the style of play that really rolled back the years. Boothroyd's approach was reminiscent of the early Graham Taylor years, playing to the strengths of his forward players. Young was quick, Henderson was strong and King was quick and strong. With booming goal kicks from Foster, on loan from Manchester United, and an eagerness to look for a forward pass first, Watford were set up to attack at home and counter-attack away.

Once the ball was rolling, they were very difficult to stop, and once they had secured a place in the play-offs, they steam-rollered Crystal Palace and Leeds United to return to the Premier League.

* * *

Even the players were a little surprised by the turnaround in fortunes. 'We had just avoided relegation, we hired a young, hungry manager no one had ever heard of, and from the players' point of view we did not think we would be promoted,' says defender Jay DeMerit. 'But Aidy Boothroyd did. The first day of pre-season training he said we were going to get promoted to the Premier League, and that confidence was bred into us.

'So, when we reached the Premier League, we still had this belief that we would be okay. Obviously, we weren't over-confident because we were going into a league that people were saying was the best, most competitive in the world. But we were an attacking team, we scored goals, we knew we would lose some games but we were not going into the league to get relegated straight away.'

Again, the task of signing players who were up to the task was difficult. Danny Shittu (£1.6m plus add-ons) and Damien Francis (£1.5m) were solid – very much so in Shittu's case – and dependable. Chris Powell was very experienced and Tommy Smith, who returned home just after the start of the season, did a good job, but the new signings did not give the impression that Watford were going for broke.

The opening game, against Everton at Goodison Park, threw up another of those incidents that seemed to favour the 'big' club. Everton led 1-0 but Watford were pressing hard for an equaliser and looked good value for a point. Chris Powell had a penalty awarded against him when the referee ruled that he had handled Tim Cahill's cross, when even someone standing on the other side of Stanley Park could tell the ball had hit Powell's head. Mikel Arteta made it 2-0 and Damien Francis's last-minute goal was no more than a consolation, rather than the equaliser it should have been. Even the BBC described it as a 'shocking penalty decision' and Boothroyd joked that he had to wait half an hour to cool down before talking to the referee.

In the next match, King gave Watford a short-lived lead

against West Ham, and that 1-1 draw suggested they might be okay, but the wait for a first league victory lasted until November 4, when Middlesbrough were beaten 2-0.

'We drew too many games and that set the tone,' says DeMerit. 'If we could have got three points earlier on it might have been different. There was a game against Fulham where we were 2-0 up and they came back at us to lead 3-2, and we saved a point with a goal in the last minute. I look back at games like that now as the ones that made the difference…'

There were the usual hard-luck stories that newly promoted teams are forced to learn by heart – the last-minute Gary Speed penalty that gave Bolton a 1-0 win, Fulham's comeback when a 2-0 win was within touching distance, Henderson's missed penalty in a 0-0 draw at Charlton. But it was the injury to King at Arsenal's Emirates Stadium that robbed the team of its line-leader, talisman and most potent threat. That 3-0 defeat at Arsenal and a 4-0 reverse at Chelsea were the only drubbings the team suffered before Christmas, but on the flip-side the win over Middlesbrough was the only league win until Blackburn were defeated on January 23.

'I rarely felt like we were totally outplayed,' says DeMerit. 'But we didn't have the killer instinct that many of the teams have. When we lost Marlon, it was very difficult to replace him. Darius had some good chances but suddenly he was on his own. We didn't have a lot of money to spend but I know Aidy wanted a deeper squad because he didn't have the chance to chop and change players. I know people think a settled team is ideal, and in a way it is, but you also need healthy competition for spots because that is really important in every team dynamic. If you know someone is after your place it keeps you consistent.

'The Premier League was totally different to the Championship, not just because of the level of the opposition but also the rhythm of the season. You play fewer games, so there's more time in between matches. You try to treat every game the same, but sometimes when you have a lot of time to prepare and you know that if you don't get a result on Saturday there's not an opportunity to put things right on Tuesday night, that feels different.

'You work hard for a week, you cover everything you possibly can, you go out and you give everything you have and you don't get the points... That is hard. You come in and look at the fixtures and think, "Holy crap, we've got these guys next week as well? How do we get something out of that?" It's what the Premier League throws at you, and even the teams that other people are taking points off are not easy.

'I think if you look, we conceded quite a lot of late goals. That was nothing to do with a lack of fitness. We were a fit group – really fit – but the mental concentration required is very tiring in another way. We weren't used to that. So, you'd dwell on that for a week, and another huge game would come along, and you knew every single point mattered and every game was being watched. That pressure builds up.'

Watford were bottom just before Christmas and only briefly raised themselves up to 19th place – like the spindly-armed guy in the Mr Muscle ads trying to do press-ups – before slipping to the foot of the table again.

In the January transfer window, Ashley Young was sold to Aston Villa for £8million, with an extra £1.65m in add-ons. It would have been impossible to turn down that sort of money but it did highlight, again, the challenges facing a club like Watford. In the 1980s, they kept hold of John Barnes for six years; Young was sold within six months of reaching the Premier League.

With all that money burning a hole in their pockets, one has to wonder whether a less scattergun approach to recruitment in January might not have been wiser. Moses Ashikodi, Lee Williamson, Will Hoskins, Steve Kabba, Yohann Cavalli, Gareth Williams, Cedric Avinel and Douglas Rinaldi all arrived that month – with only Kabba, at £500,000 from Sheffield United, and Williamson and Hoskins from Rotherham, costing significant fees. Years later we became accustomed under the Pozzos to a rash of players turning up at once and then watching as the majority were discarded, but this smacked of a manager who didn't know what he was doing. Was he trying to stay in the Premier League, or was he preparing for a subsequent promotion campaign?

At least an FA Cup run served as light relief from the week-to-week grind. A succession of relatively kind ties and an excellent 1-0 win at Upton Park saw Watford reach the semi-finals, where they were hammered 4-1 by Manchester United in a one-sided match. Had it been closer, we might have indulged in conspiracy theories that, with the first cup final at the newly rebuilt Wembley at stake, the powers-that-be would not have wanted little Watford spoiling the occasion.

'The cup run did lift us a bit,' says DeMerit. 'We could relax a bit and show we were good soccer players, and I think our performances reflected that. We never gave up in the league – as long as there are points to play for you give everything – but every game it got harder and harder to see how we'd get out of it. When you have to win every game to stay up, the odds are against you. I don't think the belief in ourselves ever went away but what I would say is how many times do you need to get kicked in the guts before you have to bend over?

'I think the stress got to Aidy a bit. He was being hyped as a future England manager, and I think he ran with that because he really believed in that, but even his confidence started to wane. He tried a lot of different things but, unlike the previous season, nothing came off for him. None of the signings worked out great but Aidy's thing was to believe in people and hope they justified that belief. If one of those guys had come in and scored five in five it would have been great.

'In the end, Aidy got frustrated. He saw his reputation slip a little bit.'

* * *

DeMerit's advice for any newly-promoted club sounds simple but he knows that in practice it is a lot harder. 'The key is to stay consistent,' he says. 'Pick up points whenever you can. You don't necessarily get all the points you deserve when you play well – we certainly didn't – so you have to scrap whenever you can. We weren't a team that had competed at the top level before, and Aidy hadn't managed at the top before. We didn't have the experience to fall back on when things were tough but I think we did a pretty good job of trying to learn on the fly.

'If I had to say anything to any defender it would be, "Remember the last 15 minutes." That's so important. Do not switch off for a single second until you hear the final whistle because if you do it can cost you. I remember against Chelsea at Vicarage Road we lost to a last-minute Solomon Kalou header. That was about the best we played all season. We had all done our jobs but we gave them one chance right at the end, they scored, and we got nothing.

'I still remember the Premier League season very fondly. I enjoyed it. My parents live in Wisconsin and they watched every game on TV. I played at some amazing grounds and I would say that was my best season in a Watford shirt. Even though we didn't get a lot of points, my personal performances were among the best in my career because I was tested by the best. It's the most I've enjoyed losing, let me put it that way.

'I enjoyed the challenge. To see Steven Gerrard spray the

ball wherever he wanted, to be close enough to see that live, that was the first time I experienced a real general on the field. He drove that Liverpool team. And to go up against Didier Drogba at that time was one of the few times in my career when I felt helpless. At least against Wayne Rooney I could compete physically but with Drogba, he was bigger than me, stronger than me, his feet were quicker and better than mine. That was the first time I was up against someone who was just way, way better than me.'

* * *

So, what does it take to stay up these days?

Forget the intangibles – the mathematics of survival are pretty clear. Modern history says that a team would be very, very unlucky to get relegated with 42 points. In the 19 seasons since the Premier League was cut to 20 teams, only West Ham in 2003 have gone down with as many.

Let's take 42 points as the target. To reach that requires ten wins and 12 draws, or 11 wins and nine draws. Either way, a very rough rule of thumb is to aim to always have more points than games played.

The toughest thing about promotion to the Premier League is that after an aspirational season spent looking upwards and ahead, it requires a mental gear-change because so much time can be consumed with glancing over shoulders and fretting about who might be catching up. And the reality is that the gravitational pull is so strong it can suck a team in, even after a good start.

But there's something to learn from Graham Taylor's first year in the top flight, when he gave the relegation threat barely a thought: 'They are all human, with two arms and two legs and some of them might not be as good as they think they are.'

3

Has there ever been a more thrilling passage of play at Vicarage Road than the dying seconds of the Hornets' play-off semi-final against Leicester?

In the time between Manuel Almunia's penalty save and Troy Deeney's finish, emotions went from hell to heaven.

The players who created one of the most beautiful memories in the club's entire history talk us through the goal from beginning to end – all 25 seconds of it...

THE DEENEY GOAL

Extra time was little more than a minute or two away. Watford and Leicester City's weary players faced another half an hour, and possibly a penalty shoot-out, to decide who would go to Wembley and keep their Premier League dream alive. The tension of a frenetic match had drained everyone inside Vicarage Road and now there was a feeling of nervous exhaustion as supporters began to prepare themselves for the mental exertion of extra time.

Deep into added time, with almost six additional minutes having been added on by the referee, Michael Oliver, there was time for one last push by the men in blue. The ball was played long, up towards the penalty area at the Vicarage Road end, and as Watford's supporters willed someone, anyone, to take control of the situation and clear the ball to safety, suddenly one of the figures in blue was inside the penalty area with the ball.

What happened next was arguably the most extraordinary sequence of play in Watford's history. In the space of a couple of minutes Watford's players and supporters experienced disaster and triumph and just about everything else in between. A penalty was awarded to Leicester. It was saved – twice – and Watford broke forward with a move of such impressive free-flowing clarity it was as if they were oblivious to the emotional maelstrom around them. The goal, the pitch invasion and the celebrations are burned indelibly into our consciousness from two perspectives – our own real-time memories, the combination of what we each saw, from wherever we were, stitched together into a perfectly imperfect showreel, and secondly the director's cut: the television coverage watched and re-watched countless times on YouTube. Don't tell me you haven't sought out that clip at times over the past couple of years, either as a pick-me-up after a bereft home performance, or as a confirmation of everything that is golden in happier times. I bet you're off to watch it now. Go on, don't let me stop you. This chapter will still be here when you get back.

* * *

Breathtaking, wasn't it? Yes, there have been goals of greater historical significance – ones that have clinched promotion, staved off relegation or confirmed a cup knock-out. Yes, there have been better goals scored by men in yellow, although not too many leap immediately to mind. But Troy Deeney's goal against Leicester City in the fading seconds of a play-off semi-final second leg on Sunday, May 12, 2013, had the perfect combination of significance and brilliance. It was a moment that justifies a lifetime's obsession – a moment you can point to that answers definitively the question: why do you support Watford?

So let's set the scene before we hear from the players. It's almost too painful to reflect on the fact that had Watford beaten Leeds United on the final day of the regular season, they'd have been promoted to the Premier League and spared the play-offs entirely. The first leg of the semi-final at Leicester was no classic. It was an open and energetic encounter but the blustery wind meant it was also scrappy and error-strewn. Only David Nugent's late header – his first goal in 17 matches, naturally – prevented a goalless draw.

The task that lay before Watford at Vicarage Road was simple. Win the game by one goal and take their chance in the penalty shoot-out, win it by two and go directly to Wembley.

For Jonathan Hogg, who had been a regular in Gianfranco Zola's midfield as a holding player charged with disrupting the opposition and giving the team's attacking forces the freedom to go forward, there was a shock in store on the eve of the match.

JONATHAN HOGG

The gaffer pulled me aside the night before the game and said: 'You've been brilliant for me this year but I need to go more positive and play a more attacking game. We need to get on top and get back into it.'

I am not known for my goals or attacking threat, so I could see what he was saying but I was absolutely gutted. It was the most important game of the season and I'm sitting on the bench. I wasn't being rested, I wasn't injured – I was being left out for a tactical reason, even though I was fit and ready to do my job. It's not easy but you need to stay professional and positive for the rest of the team.

It was a really hard watch – the hardest game I've ever had to watch. I wanted to be out on the pitch, helping the lads to win the game – not sitting on the bench. It was such a strange situation because I wanted the lads to do as well as they could so we could get to the final, but on the other hand I wanted the gaffer to see something that I could improve so he'd send me on.

After 15 minutes, Matej Vydra scored a goal fitting of the occasion, connecting with a lofted through ball from Marco Cassetti, which itself was an audacious touch with the outside of the boot. As the ball dropped over his shoulder, Vydra connected with a devastating left-foot volley that flew past Kasper Schmeichel. Now it was 1-1 on aggregate. Game on.

JONATHAN HOGG

When Matej scored the first goal, the place erupted. I'd seen him do things like that every day in training but to do it in that match was something special. For them to shoot straight back and put us back to square one was really disappointing. We had to score again, no matter what, and it was agony to watch.

I knew Fernando [Forestieri] would get on before me. If anyone can change a game, it's that fella. He could go on and change a game with a run or a touch. I used to call him the little magic man. On his day, he's unplayable, he really is.

Forestieri did go on before Hogg, in the 64th minute, and although he wasn't involved in the goal, within a minute of his arrival, Vydra had scored his second after a neat one-two with Deeney. The match was level. Twelve minutes after that, Watford had the ball in the net again following a nice run from Forestieri, a delicately slotted pass from Vydra and a measured finish from Deeney. There was only one problem: the assistant referee's flag was up for offside before Deeney even received the ball. The game was stretched, both teams were creating chances and as the clock ticked down everyone knew that the next goal would probably win the tie. With 11 minutes left, Hogg got the nod.

JONATHAN HOGG

Before I went on, the game was going from end to end. We were creating chances but so were they, and anyone could have scored. It was being played at such a pace that the gaffer wanted me to go on there and slow it down a bit, break it up in midfield, take the sting out of their attacks, win the ball and give it to Fernando or whoever.

When the gaffer gave me the thumbs up, I was as fresh as a daisy but absolutely pumped with adrenaline. It's definitely harder to go into a game and pick up the pace of it than it is to start a match. I knew that if it stayed 2-1 we'd be going to extra-time and I could give the lads a lift in the middle of the park if we had to play another half an hour.

Time was almost up. Five minutes of added time had been played. But the referee, Michael Oliver, was about to make an important decision. Incredibly, a fortnight earlier, Oliver had been the referee at Brentford's League One promotion show-down against Doncaster Rovers. The Bees needed to win to go up, Rovers needed only a draw. The game was goalless, and deep into stoppage time, when Oliver gave Brentford a penalty. Marcello Trotta hit the bar, Doncaster cleared their lines, broke quickly and James Coppinger scored to ensure they went up as champions instead of runners-up.

Leicester's French player Anthony Knockaert was running at goal when Marco Cassetti made his challenge.

TROY DEENEY

I was on the halfway line and they had a goal kick. They won the header and they got in that way. I was initially jogging back because I thought it was going to be a goal kick to us. I didn't think he was going to give a penalty in a pressure situation like that. I was stood on the halfway line as he [Knockaert] went through and

Wes Morgan [the Leicester defender] says: 'Oh, I think we're in here…' meaning that if he had stayed up, he was through on goal and could have scored.

JONATHAN HOGG

When Knockaert tried to take Marco on, I was standing just inside Marco. As Knockaert touched it across, I knew it wasn't a penalty. It was nowhere near a penalty – never. No way. When I heard the whistle, I thought the ref was going to book him for diving, but then he pointed to the spot.

MARCO CASSETTI

It was not a foul. No foul. He didn't do anything to stay on his feet. When he felt the touch, he went down like he's in the swimming pool. I made contact but not enough for a foul. It was shoulder against shoulder. It was fair. It was not a trip. The ball was going to run out. I couldn't believe it but when the referee makes that decision you can't say anything.

TROY DEENEY

That was the story of our season, really. There had been so many games before, like the Leeds match on the last day, when I got sent-off, when we should have had a penalty. Hoggy went down and we didn't get it. Five or six times that year we should have had penalties so to have one given against us for a dive was quite frustrating, as you can imagine. When the ref gave the penalty, Wes runs over to Nigel Pearson [the Leicester manager] to ask, you know, if we score, is everyone go-ing to drop back in? They're already planning for if he scores. I was stood next to one of their other defenders and I said: 'I don't know how you lot are going to win this. The first game, yeah, you nicked it, but we had our chances too, and in this game we've absolutely battered you.' He said: 'Yeah, you've played well.'

JONATHAN HOGG

I remember shouting: 'How can he give that?' At first I was thinking: 'We're done here. It's over.' I felt like crying on the pitch there and then. I was so devastated to be robbed with a penalty in the last minute. Not even the last minute – the 96th minute.

IKECHI ANYA

From my angle it looked a soft penalty. That was the worst feeling imaginable. But Manu [Manuel Almunia] was a great keeper. I thought he had a chance.

JONATHAN HOGG

I started thinking positively. 'Manu can save this.' Then: 'Manu is going to save this.' I stood and watched the penalty. I was staring at the ball, then at Almunia, then back at the ball again. Every striker fancies the penalty more than the keeper – you know the odds are with the striker – but you just hope. You have to hope, don't you? I knew Knockaert had to hit it well to score. Almunia's not just going to let it in.

IKECHI ANYA

When he saved the first one, it seemed to take Manu an eternity to get up again. It seemed like he couldn't get up. He went from super-slow-motion to really fast and stopped it again. As soon as he stopped the ball the second time and it was cleared, I turned...

TROY DEENEY

I'm watching the penalty, waiting for the net to go, and I thought, 'Oh, he's missed it... Oh, he's missed it again.' Manu makes the first save but I'm thinking how did the guy miss the second? It seems to take Manu forever to get to the second one because he kind of falls on one knee. If a goalkeeper dives fully, he can push himself back up, but he just fell on one knee and then blocked the second one with his chest. While all this is going on, my legs are still planted to the same spot. I hadn't moved because I thought it was over. The first thing I thought was: 'We've got another half an hour of this.' It was quite an intense game and quite warm and I knew I had to get my legs going again. 'I need to sort this out.'

MARCO CASSETTI

I was not certain but I knew Manu had the quality to stop the penalty. I want to say thank you to Manuel Almunia now, two years later, for saving that penalty two times.

JONATHAN HOGG

I thought Knockaert was just going to tap in the re-bound but Almunia stopped it again. How did he do that? It's a fantastic reaction. The noise was just unbelievable. Then Marco smashed it away...

MARCO CASSETTI

I was first to the ball. I cleared the box. I wanted to get it away from our box because I thought the match was done. We had played 96 minutes; now we have to play 30 minutes more.

JONATHAN HOGG

For Anya to bring the ball out of the sky like that…
What a touch. What a touch that was under pressure.
It's the last minute of the game, he's just seen the penalty saved, the crowd are going bananas and he takes it
down like that.

TROY DEENEY

How has he done that? The ball didn't move, did it?
It stopped dead on the end of his foot. What a great
touch.

IKECHI ANYA

I was buzzing after the penalty save. There was a big
roar and we were still alive. I never really thought my
touch was that good until people started telling me it
was. I just wanted to get it under control. Let's run at
them. Their players are out of position.

FERNANDO FORESTIERI

When Almunia saves the ball, I start to run. Then when
Anya controls the ball, I start to sprint in case he wants
to pass to me.

TROY DEENEY

If you watch, I've not moved far. Ikechi's running past
me and plays it down the line to Nando and I know I
need to start moving, so I am jogging, jogging, jogging,
just seeing how it goes.

JONATHAN HOGG

As soon as Anya brought the ball down and started
driving forward, I thought: 'I am going to break my

neck to get into the box here.' I thought I could time my run nicely, get round the back without anyone picking me up...

IKECHI ANYA

Hoggy starts running from their box to ours. I wasn't really thinking. The normal players' instinct is to get forward.

MARCO CASSETTI

Our philosophy was to keep possession and attack. This is how the gaffer wanted us to play: to attack quickly.

IKECHI ANYA

I gave the ball to Fernando on the edge of the pitch. He stays wide and I carry on running, just inside, in case he wants to do a one-two.

TROY DEENEY

Normally, Nando is one of those who comes back, comes back, takes a few touches, but here he's taken two touches and put it in the box. By now I know that I really need to get into the box.

FERNANDO FORESTIERI

The pass [from Anya] came perfectly. When I was running, I knew where Hoggy and Troy were going to be. I'm lucky because it's a good cross...

MARCO CASSETTI

Me and Hoggy were the only two who didn't score that season – well, the only two who played a lot of games.

Every day in training we joked about it.

JONATHAN HOGG

We had a bit of banter about it. Before matches we'd say: 'Who's going to score today?' Before that game, Marco said to me: 'You're going to score.'

TROY DEENEY

As the ball is going over to Hoggy, I thought: 'He's not going to try to score with that, is he?'

JONATHAN HOGG

What happens now? The ball is coming across and out of the corner of my eye, I saw Kasper Schmeichel jump in a big star shape with his arms and legs out. I saw a defender run to cover the line and in that split-second I thought: 'It's got to be a hell of a header to get over the keeper and over the defender.' I heard Troy screaming at me so, being the unselfish man I am, I let him take all the glory!

TROY DEENEY

I was jogging in and there were five or six Leicester players there in and around the box but they were in shock. It was kind of six v six and naturally the defenders were trying to cover the goal, so they ran in, which left me with a bit of space.

JONATHAN HOGG

I can just see Troy coming onto it and in a way the header has got to be like a little pass to him. I didn't want a big looping header that bounces up around his chest. It's got to be a nice cushioned header to give him

the best possible chance. I steered it downwards, tried
to take the pace off the ball and just set it up nicely…

TROY DEENEY

I saw Vydra coming in, so I was screaming: 'Troy's!'
Vydra jumped out of the way. I was just hanging back.
Where's Hoggy going to put it? How will it come off
his head? What if it bounces there? I wanted to give
myself the best amount of space so I could see where
the ball was going to go. I didn't have time to think but
with Gianfranco Zola we did loads of shooting drills in
training. We never set the ball up so it was rolling nicely
– we worked on ugly set-ups, where the ball is bouncing
or it's a bit high or off to the side or whatever. Very
rarely in a game does the ball fall perfectly for you, so
we tried to create match situations in training. We'd
done seven or eight months of preparation for that
moment. It wasn't as easy as it sounds. I just wanted
to keep it from going over. I wanted to keep it down
and on target. It was kind of like a free shot because if
I missed, we still had extra time. Time was going slow
but I was just watching the ball. Schmeichel nearly got
a touch to it but I hit it that well, even if he had got a
touch it would have gone in.

IKECHI ANYA

I had the best angle to see him score. As soon as I saw
him strike it, I knew it was going in. The event has
eclipsed how good a finish that was. The euphoria of
the moment has overtaken the actual technique.

JONATHAN HOGG

Take the circumstances, the atmosphere and all that

into account and it's an absolute peach of a strike. It could have bounced awkwardly and hit his shin but he struck it so cleanly.

TROY DEENEY

Don't ask me why the shirt came off. The euphoria came over me, obviously with the start to the season I had. I was in prison and it didn't look like I was even going to come back and play. I had my family there, my brother, my friends. As soon as I scored, I didn't see anyone else – I just saw where they were and ran to them. They had the same mentality as me. As soon as I scored they thought: 'We're going to him.' They're climbing towards the seats and I jump over the advertising boards. I didn't realise how big a gap there was behind there, so it's a good job my brother caught me. I was totally caught up in the moment.

JONATHAN HOGG

The place just erupted. Wow. I have never experienced anything like that. I was still back-pedalling a bit from the header. Troy took his top off and I'm just chasing him as fast I could. It was the best feeling I've ever had in a football match. Ever. Ten seconds ago we thought we were out; all of a sudden we're going to Wembley.

FERNANDO FORESTIERI

The fans came onto the pitch and I took my shirt off and gave it to one of them and he said: 'No, no, you need this. You still have to play.'

TROY DEENEY

I didn't know the gaffer had slipped over celebrating

the goal. I didn't know we still had 30 seconds to play
or whatever. Someone was shouting we had to get
the fans off the pitch. I had thrown my shirt into the
crowd but I clocked who'd caught it and I was like: 'I
need it back.' They chucked the shirt and I put it on.
There was a line of police across the halfway line and as
I got back into our half of the pitch, Almunia was next
to me. He thought it was over as well. I said: 'Shouldn't
you be in goal?'

JONATHAN HOGG

It was a good job the fans all came onto the pitch
because we needed that time to calm down. We had a
four- or five-minute break to just concentrate. There
was only 30 seconds left but it wasn't done.

TROY DEENEY

I asked the ref how long we had left but I don't think
he answered. I knew they were going to hit it long so
we had to be strong. I said that if we got it, to just get
it into the corner and I'll chase it and try to hold it. I
think Harry Kane fouled Manu and that was it. Maybe
there was a bit longer to go but the ref called it a day.

MARCO CASSETTI

We cleared the pitch and played the last 30 seconds, and
then the emotion hit me. You play a game like this for
the fans. The emotion was very, very strong. I've never
felt anything like it in my whole career – not even when
I scored in the Champions League for Roma.

JONATHAN HOGG

We celebrated after the game. I can't describe how

special that was. Feeling part of that team, all laughing and joking and jumping around. Zola said to me: 'Hoggy, that assist counts as ten goals.' Every now and then I see that goal on TV and the lads at Huddersfield say: 'I didn't realise that was you.' It was definitely, by a long chalk, the best thing I've experienced in my life.

TROY DEENEY

It's good to watch it every now and then and I can appreciate it more now. Back then, I was doing my job. You know, that's what I'm supposed to do. It's nice to have scored that goal but I have more to do. When I'm older I can look back on it. Even though we went on to lose to Crystal Palace in the final, the fans still have that day. But really, now, while I'm still playing, I want to get to the Premier League. That goal does prove that it's never done until it's done. That goal shows the magic and beauty of football. It's why we love it, for moments like that.

JONATHAN HOGG

If you'd said to me that my final game for Watford would be at Wembley, I'd not have believed you. It was a totally different feeling. I don't think we turned up. When we were at our best, the quality, the pace, the shape and the organisation of our game was so good. It was a really disappointing day and I can't really put my finger on why we didn't play.

MARCO CASSETTI

I feel so sad because I made the decisive foul in the final against Crystal Palace. I've been sad for two years about that. It was the big final – Wembley, 85,000

people – and we didn't do what we could do. We didn't
play like Watford in the regular season. Crystal Palace
did their best: they did more than us and they deserved
it. When [Wilfried] Zaha was running at me, I wanted
to put the ball out for a throw-in. But he is the worst
player to have against you. It was extra time. I was tired,
eh? I went to try to kick the ball off but he anticipat-
ed and touched the ball away so I touched him. Yeah,
yeah, it was a foul. I can't say the same thing about the
penalty against Knockaert but this one was a foul. We
wanted to get to the Premier League so much. It was
very disappointing and I think the next season we lost
something. After Zola left, we needed to start again
and it was difficult. But even now I always look for
the results and hope that Watford win and can reach
the Premier League, even though I won't be there with
them.

This chapter is titled *The Deeney Goal* but really it was a goal
that belonged to everyone. The team, the supporters, everyone inside Vicarage Road that afternoon (bar a few thousand in
blue) and plenty of people further afield. If one moment was
needed to sum up the appeal of the entire sport, and what it is
to be a football supporter, that would be a contender.

Everything that followed Deeney's shot lives on in the
memories of those who witnessed it – the pitch invasion,
Gianfranco Zola losing his cool momentarily and sprinting
down the touchline before slipping over, the celebrations that
lasted long into the evening. Then there were the opportunities
to re-live it – videos of Sky's coverage posted online and the
soon-to-be immortal line, 'Do not scratch your eyes.'

That Watford fell short at Wembley hurt, of course, and it
mattered deeply at the time, but as the wounds from that defeat

faded, the memory of Deeney's goal remained strong.

And it the memory of moments like this that strengthens the bond between a club and its supporters. Within six months, Zola had gone. Two years on, as Watford reached the Premier League, Almunia, Briggs, Cassetti and Chalobah had all departed. Sooner or later, they will all move on but they will always share that moment.

It was interesting, during the course of conducting the interviews for this chapter, how some players found it more difficult than others to recall the details of that goal. You'd think, given the dramatic significance of it, that the memories would be seared into the brain, but that is perhaps to misunderstand the mindset of professional sportspeople. They think about today and tomorrow and the past is something that gets locked away, only to be indulged when they pack in the game.

Moments like that are special because there could have been a hundred different outcomes had any of the players involved chosen to act differently. Cassetti could have smashed the ball off the pitch for a throw-in. Anya could have mis-controlled the ball. Forestieri could have run into a challenge and lost possession. Hogg could have chosen to play safe and hold his position in the middle of the pitch. And Denney could have fired the ball high, wide and handsome.

None of those things happened but one wonders if, somewhere in a parallel universe, Anthony Knockaert tucked away his penalty...

4

In 1983, Watford qualified for the Uefa Cup – the competition that became the Europa League.

Having just missed out on seeing the Hornets play in Europe, it has become something of an obsession for this writer over the past three decades.

There has not been a realistic chance to play in Europe since, unless you count the Anglo-Italian Cup, but Watford's promotion back to the Premier League has sparked dreams of flying to some far-flung European city to see the Hornets in action.

To be honest, it doesn't even have to be that far away. A ferry ride and a drive would do, as long as it's for a match in a proper European cup.

DREAMING OF WAALWIJK

The summer of 1999 felt like it lasted an eternity, although the close-season break between competitive matches was actually the shortest in the club's history. Just 67 blank days separated the play-off final win over Bolton at Wembley on May 31 and the opening game of the Premiership season against Wimbledon on August 7 but, boy, did that summer drag on. There wasn't even a World Cup or European Championships to fill the void, transfer activity was relatively thin on the ground and, once the fixture list had been published, time seemed to stand still, such was the excitement and anticipation.

With time on my hands, my mind began to wander and I started dreaming of Waalwijk, or Lech Poznan, or HJK Helsinki. I started to think about the away goals rule, extra-time and penalties, of 30-hour round trips by plane, train or coach to the Netherlands, Poland or Finland. I imagined swapping shirts or scarves with Jan, Jacek or Jari and the sight of flags reading 'Norfolk Hornets' or 'Watford On Tour' draped over fences and terraces in some far-flung ground.

You will note that I wasn't dreaming of Juventus, Barcelona or Bayern Munich (I wasn't unrealistic) but Watford's promotion to the Premiership had expanded my horizons enough to dream of a place in the Intertoto Cup – more of which later.

Let me explain how this flight of fantasy started.

You see, I narrowly missed out on witnessing Watford's one and only European campaign in the autumn of 1983. The

Uefa Cup matches pre-dated my debut at Vicarage Road by a couple of months but, having said that, even if I'd been a regular attendee of Saturday afternoon home games, I would almost certainly not have gone to midweek evening matches because I was only eight years old. I know eight-year-olds go to evening kick-offs these days but this was a more conservative era, when bed time meant bed time and there was no such thing as staying up until midnight playing FIFA 2015 with the sound turned down. Come to think of it, children grow up so fast these days that eight-year-olds probably think nothing of a Wednesday night trip to Zenit St Petersburg. On their own.

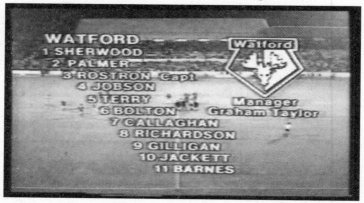

Anyway, the European adventure was over by the time I got to Vicarage Road and all I had to go on were the newspaper reports, photographs in the match programme and, later, an end-of-season highlights video.

On there was BBC's Sportsnight coverage of the home leg against Kaiserslautern in the first round, complete with John Motson's commentary, and some shakier, home-video-style footage of the Levski Spartak and Sparta Prague home games shot on a video camera from a gantry on top of the old Shrodells stand. Incidentally, that's a video tape I still have, long, long

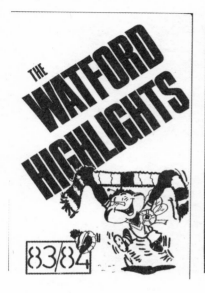

WATFORD HIGHLIGHTS _ 1983/84

VERSUS

COVENTRY
IPSWICH
NOTTS COUNTY
KAISERLAUTERN
TOTTENHAM
LEVSKI SPARTEK
HUDDERSFIELD
LEICESTER
PRAGUE
NOTTS FOREST
ASTON VILLA
BIRMINGHAM CITY
STOKE
W.B.A.
BRIGHTON
EVERTON
Q.P.R.
SUNDERLAND
NOTTS COUNTY (AWAY)

55 mins   49 goals

after getting rid of my last video recorder.

At the risk of sounding like an old fuddy-duddy, the kids today don't know they're born, with their complaining about being last to be shown on the Football League highlights show, which, by the time you read this, will no doubt have become a complaint about being shown last on Match of the Day. Imagine having to wait until the following Christmas to see clips of the season's goals on video?

To be fair, Watford were well ahead of their time in 1983. They videoed all their home games and supporters could buy copies of each full match for £10, plus £1 postage and packaging. Considering it cost £2.50 to stand on the Vicarage Road terrace, it didn't represent staggeringly good value for money, especially when you had to supply your own VHS or BetaMax tape too. For anyone who's baffled by what all this means, videos were what preceded DVDs. If you're not sure what a

DVD is, it's basically Netflix on a disc.

Years later, I bought the programmes from the three away European ties – Kaiserslautern in West Germany, Levski Spartak in Bulgaria and Sparta Prague in Czechoslovakia. I could not read German or Czech, and I had no hope of deciphering the Cyrillic characters of the Levski Spartak programme, but just to see them and imagine what it was like for those lucky supporters who joined the European travel club, or made their own way to the games, and picked up one of these soon-to-be pieces of history was a pleasure.

In volume two of *Tales from the Vicarage*, Mike Walters wrote so evocatively about his own journey to Sofia for the most unlikely away win in the club's history, and the players who were part of the adventure remembered how every game, home or away, was a voyage into the unknown.

The team that played in Europe looked very different to the

one that had finished runners-up the previous season. Luther Blissett had accepted the chance of a lifetime and had moved to AC Milan, although he made the trip to West Germany to sit among the Hornets supporters for their first-ever European tie. Gerry Armstrong and Ross Jenkins had also left. And injuries had hit the squad hard, meaning Taylor had to press some very young, inexperienced players into European action. As he remarked, more than once, the team that played in Europe was half the reserve team.

But they did the club, and themselves, proud. The players I spoke to about the European matches for *Enjoy the Game* had so many memories. Jimmy Gilligan recalled the fervent crowd packed into Kaiserslautern's compact Betzenberg stadium, and the horns, hooters and flares spewing red smoke into the sky that created a typically 'European' atmosphere. Gilligan made history, by scoring Watford's first European goal in the 3-1 defeat in West Germany.

Graham Taylor sensed that Kaiserslautern thought the tie was dead when they arrived at Vicarage Road wearing jeans, t-shirts and tracksuits instead of club suits and ties. He sensed a casual complacency about the more illustrious opponents, some of whom had World Cup and European Championship experience. Watford decided to set about them with pace, energy and aggression, and it paid off. Watford were 2-0 up inside ten minutes – level on aggregate and with the advantage of the away goal they'd scored in West Germany. In the second half, Ian Richardson – Gilligan's reserve-team strike partner – scored his second of the game and, late on, Taylor sent his coach John Ward round to the other side of the pitch from the bench to encourage and coach the players on that side through the final 10 or 15 minutes (something that was technically not allowed, because all the coaching staff had to stay on the bench, but they got away with it).

The second round paired Watford with the Bulgarian side, Levski Spartak. The first leg was drawn, which, with an away match in front of 60,000 still to come, should have spelled the end of the adventure. Taylor sent his coach Steve Harrison to Sofia to watch Levski, but his hosts gave him a team sheet with the line-ups written in Cyrillic, which wasn't much use to him. Harrison reported back: 'Well, gaffer, all I can tell you is that the blond lad and the fella at the back are both good players.'

The away leg must go down as one of the most extraordinary upsets Watford have ever pulled off. Forget beating Manchester United at Old Trafford – this was another level. The city was grey, with Soviet-style tower blocks and queues at the shops. The food was unpalatable – Neil Price remembers a bowl of watery vegetable soup with a hard boiled egg in it and tough, chewy meat – and the atmosphere in the stadium was hostile. Add to that the fact Levski were awarded two penalties in the first half (they scored the first and missed the second) and the odds were stacked against the young Hornets.

I'd not seen any footage of that game, until some showed up on YouTube (it's still there). Although it's not great quality film, I appreciated for the first time how good Nigel Callaghan's equaliser was – a searing right-foot shot that flew into the net from outside the box. That goal was second in the goal of the season competition that year – beaten by John Barnes' brilliant trick, dribble and dipping volley against Birmingham City in the FA Cup quarter-final – but if anything, Callaghan's strike is better and it probably would have won had more people seen it.

There were some very famous teams in the draw for the third round – Bayern Munich, Internazionale, Celtic and Anderlecht – but Watford got a bad draw. They were to face Sparta Prague. The Czech side were not quite as glamorous as some of the others, but they were a very good team, and, with the second leg due to be played on December 7, just as the winter was beginning to bite, it would be a very tricky trip.

The first leg was lost 3-2, leaving a mountain to climb away from home. All the players talked of how the pitch that night was frozen solid and, had it not been a European tie, it would surely have been postponed, but it was not until I saw some clips on YouTube that I realised how bad the pitch had been. Even on the grainy film it's possible to see icy white grooves running the full length of the pitch. Sparta Prague were used to playing on such surfaces. Watford had no chance and lost 4-0.

* * *

My fascination with the Uefa Cup run started early. I can remember saying, after one of my first matches at Vicarage Road: 'Dad, where did Watford play the Uefa Cup games?'

'One was in West Germany, one was in Bulgaria and the other one was in Czechoslovakia.'

'No, I mean the home games.'

'Here, at Vicarage Road.'

That's right, I hadn't realised that a team played its European home games at 'home' but, in my defence, there's a lot to take in during those early months after falling in love with football. There are nicknames and ground names to learn, lists of league champions, FA Cup winners and World Cup hosts to commit to memory. I couldn't pick up everything at once.

Missing the matches contributed to my sense of there being loose ends to tie up but it also struck me that if Watford had just had a slice of luck, they might have made it to the Uefa Cup final.

That autumn, Graham Taylor had been steadily rebuilding the team – replacing Blissett and Jenkins with Maurice Johnston and George Reilly, adding David Bardsley and Lee Sinnott at the back, and doing such a skilled transplant job that Watford reached the FA Cup final at the end of the season. The great unanswered question is how Watford would have done if those four, and the others who were injured, had been able to play. Johnston and Reilly forged such a potent partnership so quickly that they could have taken Europe by storm. Unfortunately they had been signed too late, after the European registration deadline, to play against Sparta Prague, but they would have been eligible for the quarter-finals had Watford got through.

In my own mind, had Watford beaten Sparta Prague, they would have beaten Hajduk Split in the last eight to set up an

all-English semi-final against Tottenham Hotspur. I was confident that, over two legs, Watford would beat Spurs and would
have faced Anderlecht in the final.

My theory was developed early. In fact, I can remember
telling a Spurs supporter at school, shortly before the second
leg of the final, that it should have been Watford, not them,
facing Anderlecht. His response may have been to push me
into a bush at the bottom of the playing fields but that doesn't
change the fact I was undoubtedly right.

Spurs beat Anderlecht on penalties at White Hart Lane after
drawing both legs 1-1. But it could all have been so different. It
could have been Watford, although the Hornets would probably have got the job done without needing penalties.

* * *

The wait for another campaign has stretched to 32 years now.
In that time, Southampton, Queens Park Rangers, Norwich
City, Leicester City, Ipswich, Fulham, Bolton, Wigan, Birmingham – even Millwall, for heaven's sake – have played in Europe.
If you count the Intertoto Cup, which, of course, I do, you can
add Wimbledon, Crystal Palace and Bradford City too. Supporters of some of these clubs may scoff at the suggestion that
they are comparable to Watford but they are and it proves that
Watford can dream of playing in Europe again.

My obsession, for that is what it became, began in the
immediate aftermath of the FA Cup final defeat against Everton in May 1984. It was disappointing enough not to win the
cup but when I realised that it also meant there would be no
return to Wembley for a Charity Shield game against league
champions Liverpool and no place in the European Cup Winners' Cup, I was disconsolate. The following May, Everton beat
Rapid Vienna to win the now-defunct European trophy and

again, as I watched on television, I couldn't help thinking it could, and should, have been Watford in Rotterdam that night.

The route into Europe had been blocked that season by Luton in the FA Cup and Sunderland, who knocked us out of the Milk Cup at the quarter-final stage. The reward for Norwich City, the eventual cup winners, who beat Sunderland at Wembley, was a place in the 1985-86 Uefa Cup, although they were unable to take it up because by then English clubs had been banned from European competition after the Heysel stadium riot involving some Liverpool supporters.

And so, the European dream faded for a few years and, by the time English clubs were re-admitted to Europe in 1990, Watford had been relegated from the top flight.

* * *

It's probably inaccurate to say there was a buzz of excitement in 1992 when it was announced that the Anglo-Italian Cup was being revived. This had been a short-lived competition in the early 1970s and had been won by Swindon, Blackpool, Newcastle and AS Roma. After a short break it returned as a competition between semi-professional clubs, with Sutton United the sole 'Anglo' victors in its ten years.

The formation of the Premier League meant the end of the unpopular Full Members Cup, which had been open to all clubs in the top two divisions, although routinely ignored by the biggest clubs. There have been many consequences of the formation of the Premier League, not all of them good, but the demise of the Full Members Cup was nothing to lament.

The Football League and the clubs in Italy's second division, Serie B, came up with this exotic replacement and although some critics quickly dubbed it as the mousiest of Mickey Mouse cups, I was not one of them. This, I sensed, could be Watford's route back into Europe. Okay, not proper Europe, but Italy was definitely abroad.

For that first competition in 1992-93, the 24 clubs in the renamed First Division (now the Championship) were drawn in eight regional groups of three. The winners of each group would progress to a second phase where they would meet four Italian qualifiers from Serie B in another group phase, playing two matches at home and two away. The results would count towards two mini leagues – an English table and an Italian table, with the top sides in each group facing each other in two-legged all-English and all-Italian semi-finals. I hope you're keeping up with this at the back.

This rather convoluted format was to ensure that the final was contested by one English team and one Italian team but it also meant that anyone hoping to win the Anglo-Italian Cup would have to negotiate nine matches – more than it takes to win the FA Cup. Looking back, it was all a preposterous waste of time.

Not that I thought that when the draw for the first group gave Watford an away game at Bristol City and a home game against the old enemy, Luton Town, in group five of the preliminary round. Steve Perryman's Watford lost 1-0 at Ashton Gate and were eliminated when they were held 0-0 at home by Luton a couple of weeks later in front of a surprisingly large crowd of 5,197 – a thousand or so more than turned up to watch a League Cup tie against Reading the following Tuesday.

The following season, Watford were again drawn in the preliminary group with Luton, with Southend making up the numbers. The Luton game at Vicarage Road took place only a fortnight after a fiery affair at Kenilworth Road on the opening day of the season. Watford had Barry Ashby and Jason Drysdale sent off in a 2-1 defeat, so this was a chance for revenge. The new stand at the Vicarage Road end was still being finished and had not been granted its safety certificate in time for the start of the season, so, for the opening few weeks, the shallow Rookery end terrace, which offered terrible views of the pitch, was the temporary home end.

Watford had not beaten Luton for six years before that night but goals from Bruce Dyer and Alex Inglethorpe clinched a 2-1 win and kept my dreams of Ascoli, Ancona, Pescara and Padova alive. As I walked away from the ground that night, discussing the game with a friend and commenting on how nice it was to actually beat Luton, a Hatters fan overheard us and said: 'Don't get too excited lads – it's in a competition that doesn't matter.'

'Matters enough for you to bother coming down here, though, doesn't it?' my friend replied.

And so, all roads led to Roots Hall. With Luton already knocked out, Watford needed only a draw to top the group and clinch a place in the 'international' phase of the competition. The official crowd that night was 1,881, although it felt like fewer. Eighteen Eighty One, which is ironic, now I look back. If more than 75 other Watford fans shared my dream of Europe, I'd be surprised.

Southend won 3-0, naturally, and I can remember the surprise on my travelling companion's face at what he felt was completely irrational anger at being knocked out of a competition that meant almost nothing. The game itself had all the buzz of a pre-season friendly; the Anglo-Italian Cup was a tinpot thing and that Luton fan had been right – it really didn't matter.

I wanted to say, 'But… but… but try telling that to the Derby fans who reached last year's final.'

I wanted to say, 'Don't you want to go to go to Brescia or Pisa or Cosenza?'

I wanted to say, 'Fiorentina are in it this year, and they've won Serie A in the past!'

Southend went on to play Fiorentina away, and hopefully the 3-0 defeat spoiled their two-day trip to Florence. They
also won at Cosenza and beat Padova 5-2 at home, which was
enough to qualify for the semi-finals as the best-placed English
team in their group. (There'd been another baffling tweak to
the competition format, presumably because it had not been
confusing enough the first year.) The Shrimpers lost to Notts
County in the semi-final, who themselves went on to lose to
Brescia at Wembley in the final. One of Notts County's defenders at Wembley that day was Charlie Palmer, who had played for
Watford against Kaiserslautern and Levski Spartak in 1983.
Clearly the European experience had stood him in good stead...

* * *

And so, dreams of a European tour were grounded for
another few years, until promotion to the Premiership in 1999
and that summer spent imagining that history might repeat
itself, although ambitions had been lowered somewhat by the
creation of the Champions League, which wasn't designed for
the likes of us. The Uefa Cup might be within reach with a
good cup run but the most realistic route was offered by the
Intertoto Cup – a competition so pointless and dreary that it
made the Anglo-Italian Cup look good.

Revived in the mid-1990s by a Uefa sub-committee that
probably met in a broom cupboard at their Swiss headquarters,
the competition was actually a response to the break-up of the
Soviet Union and other eastern European countries who now
had their own autonomous leagues. When the competition first
started, Tottenham were one of the qualifiers and, after being
told they'd be docked points if they refused to take part, fielded
a team made up of loan players and kids from the youth team
because the fixtures started in late June and they didn't want

to curtail the summer for their first-teamers. They didn't even want to soil the White Hart Lane pitch with this nonsense so they played their group games at Brighton's Goldstone Ground instead, although the official reason was that they were repairing the pitch after the London Monarchs American football team had played on it.

When Watford got promoted to the Premiership, the prospect of qualifying for the Intertoto Cup was a very real one, and that offered a route into 'proper' Europe, as West Ham showed by winning one of the finals (there were often multiple finals, all offering a place in the Uefa Cup) in 1999.

The qualifying criteria for the Intertoto Cup was suitably vague. Teams that finished just outside the Uefa Cup places were offered an entry but if they rejected the opportunity they seemed to keep asking until someone said yes. There were also places for winning the Fair Play League, so early in the 1999-2000 season I kept a keen eye on Watford's disciplinary record and in the back of my mind thought that each yellow and red card was denting our hopes.

As it turned out, Watford were relegated and it was Bradford City, who stayed up by the skin of their teeth, who qualified for the Intertoto Cup, and played RKC Waalwijk in the third round, winning 3-0 on aggregate. So, it hadn't been a silly fantasy after all. It really could have happened.

* * *

Over the next few years, any realistic route into Europe for Watford was via the back door. In 2003, before the FA Cup semi-final against Southampton at Villa Park, we stood in the concourse with a beer watching Arsenal knock Sheffield United out of the other semi-final. Knowing Arsenal were certain to qualify for the Champions League, I couldn't help saying: 'Well, if we beat Southampton today we're definitely in Europe next season.' We lost and Southampton were knocked out of the first round of the Uefa Cup by Steaua Bucharest. I'll be honest, that would have more than done for me.

A few years later, I had the same thought when the four balls went into the bowl for the semi-final draw. I wanted to avoid Manchester United and Chelsea and get Blackburn, not just because it gave Watford the best chance of making it to Wembley, but because Europe would be a certainty if we could reach the final, as the other two would be in the Champions League.

Perhaps it's a silly obsession but I live in the hope of seeing Watford in Europe one day. The odds have swung in our favour since the arrival of the Pozzos and promotion back to the Premier League. Staying up is the priority, of course – I know that – but that doesn't stop me thinking about the possibility of Europe. The Intertoto Cup is no more but the Europa League seems to let pretty much anyone in these days. We're only a good cup run or a decent disciplinary record away from getting in, as Stoke, Wigan, Hull and West Ham have shown in recent years.

And if it were to happen, I don't care where the draw takes us – Tallinn is supposed to be nice, University College Dublin would be fun, or how about Go Ahead Eagles perhaps? I've always fancied a trip to Go Ahead. (I'm joking – they play in Deventer, in the Netherlands, although I had to look that up.)

I'm not fussy, really. All I want is to say I've seen Watford play in Europe. And pre-season friendlies don't count.

5

When Watford allocated squad numbers for the first time in 1999, there was no question who would be given the number nine shirt.

Because anyone who wanted to take it from Tommy Mooney would have had a fight on their hands.

Mooney joined the Hornets on loan, when his career at Southend was going nowhere. His work-rate struck a chord and he came to embody the spirit of the fans on the pitch. He would do anything for the team, and even spent a season playing in defence.

But it was his goals in the run to the play-off final that sealed his place in the club's history and made him a Hornets hero for ever more.

SUPER TOMMY MOONEY

Troy Deeney was a raw but powerful 19-year-old who had made just one appearance for the Walsall first team when Tommy Mooney joined the Saddlers in July 2007. By this time, Mooney was at the opposite end of his career, a month away from his 36th birthday and about to begin his final season in English football before a brief swansong in the Spanish sunshine with Marbella.

Mooney's debut for Walsall was on the opening day of the season: Saturday, August 11, 2007, against Carlisle United in League One. He scored the equaliser in a match that ended as a 1-1 draw. There's nothing particularly remarkable about that except that eight minutes from the end Deeney came on as a substitute for Mooney's strike partner, Carlos Carneiro. No one would have known it at the time, but they were watching Vicarage Road heroes past and future play alongside each other.

There's more. Carlisle's centre forward that afternoon was Danny Graham, and he was joined in the second half by their substitute, Joe Garner. For a few minutes, before Graham himself was replaced, four strikers who between them embody the ups, downs and uncertainty of more than two decades in the Hornets' history were all on the Bescot Stadium pitch.

You don't need to tell Tommy Mooney about the crazy little coincidences that football throws up. His career is peppered with them, as we shall see, and for him they all seem to lead back to Vicarage Road.

Mooney signed for Walsall chiefly because their manager was Richard Money, who had been the youth team manager when Mooney was starting out at Aston Villa in the late 1980s. 'It went full circle,' he says. 'I'd played for Richard when I first started and then I ended my career in England with him.

'When I arrived at Walsall, Richard said: "We've got this lad. He's very raw, but you're quite similar." I took that to mean brawn, power and very little technique,' Mooney says with a laugh. 'Actually, he was being complimentary because Troy was a little bit better than I expected. He was a massive Birmingham fan, with this massive Birmingham City tattoo on his calf – which does mean there's no chance of him signing for Aston Villa. Richard asked me to be Troy's mentor. We played a few games together but it was more a case of helping him in training and working on a few things that I'd learned in my career.

'By the time I'd got to 36, 37, I was doing things that Watford supporters hadn't seen me do. As you get older, you get a little bit more refined because it can't all be about hustle and bustle. You have to work on your technique because your movement goes. You have to use your brain a bit more, and if you can teach a young player to use his brain as well as his strength, you can help them improve.'

Mooney and Deeney have kept in touch since. When speculation that Deeney might move to the Premier League reached its peak in the summer of 2014, he asked his former mentor for a bit of advice, and when he overtook Mooney in the all-time list of Watford's leading goalscorers in the autumn, he couldn't resist sending a text. 'Yeah, we had a laugh about that but I am proud of him,' says Mooney. 'He was a good lad even at 19. He has made a mistake [referring to Deeney's prison sentence] but he has learned from it and he's reaping the rewards now. He's worked very hard physically. He hasn't got a great deal of pace, although he is quicker than I was, but he is very strong over five yards and, even if the defender is quicker, if he gets in front he's very, very difficult to stop. But I see him now, working for the team, closing down defenders, chasing lost causes, and encouraging the younger players, as captain of the team, and it makes me very proud. He's made mistakes, sure, but he's become a good man. He's a good man, a leader, and you can't coach that into someone; you either have it or you don't. He's come a long way and he deserves the success.'

* * *

Working for the team, closing down defenders, chasing lost causes. Mooney could almost be talking about himself there, although he is honest in appraising his own shortcomings.

Later in our conversation, he says: 'I was slow, I was cumbersome. Let's be honest, if I'd been right-footed, I'd never have been a footballer because there are thousands of them, but left-footers are different. I say that to left-footed players now. I found a little niche playing in the gap between the centre back, who is a big strong fella, and the full-back, who is not. If I can pull onto the full-back, I should be stronger and then I could get in behind. I got really good at it under GT [Graham Taylor]. Before, I'd always played directly against the centre back, which is what you think you have to do as a number nine, but GT's formations were really good for me. We weren't 4-4-2, or 4-4-3 – it was more flexible than that, but we worked on it. The full back hit the diagonal up to me, I'd pull onto the full back and win it, and we'd create chances.

'There were a lot of long, monotonous training sessions under the Gaffer,' Mooney says referring to Taylor as such repeatedly, 'but when that whistle went on a Saturday, we knew exactly what we had to do and that got us success.'

Mooney's praise for Taylor is effusive, as is his own willingness to accept that the Premier League was, perhaps, a step too far for him. 'I got to a point in my career when I realised that I was a good, good Championship player. I could score goals and make a difference in games at that level. I think that's where Troy and I are different. He's desperate to go on and see what he can do against the best teams and the best defenders, and he's earned the right to do that now.'

Deeney may be a slightly different type of player but he wears the number nine that Mooney made his own during a goalscoring run that in the spring of 1999 fired Watford into a play-off place that had seemed unlikely.

When Watford were promoted to the top flight at the end of that season, they had to allocate squad numbers for the first time, abandoning the old 1-11 in favour of system that showed you were part of the elite.

In a way, Mooney was Watford's 'first' number nine. After all, when it came to dishing out the shirt numbers, there was only ever one candidate for it. 'There was no way anyone else was having it, that's for sure. That shirt was mine,' he says with a laugh.

Whatever Mooney's shortcomings, he more than made up for them with his commitment and never-say-die attitude. He never shirked from responsibility, never gave less than his all – 'I wasn't good enough not to try my best every game' – and in his seven years at Vicarage Road he assumed the role of fans' representative on the pitch. This is not to damn him with faint praise but the reason Mooney was so popular was because he played the game the way any supporter would if they ever had the chance to pull on the golden jersey. He wasn't the badge-kissing type; he didn't go in for superficial shows of affection or commitment. He rolled his sleeves up – sometimes literally, often metaphorically – and he put his body on the line for the cause. If Watford were trailing but battling to get back into a game, he'd clench his fists in the direction of the fans and urge them to get behind the team. And it only worked because they saw in Mooney the same determination and desire that he was imploring the supporters to show.

It probably speaks volumes that Mooney won the first of his two player-of-the-season awards in 1995-96, when Watford were relegated back to the lower divisions for the first time since 1979. Very few players showered themselves in glory that year but Mooney was one of those who refused to give in.

And so, when the crowd chants, 'Deeney! Deeney!', bowing down in reverence to the current number nine, it's sometimes impossible not to cast the mind back to when that chant sounded very similar: 'Mooney! Mooney!'

We meet at The Belfry – the hotel at the golf course that has hosted several Ryder Cups. It's not far from Aston Villa's Bodymoor Heath training ground, where Mooney worked as the club's loan manager, co-ordinating loan moves for Villa's young players and making sure they were benefiting from the experience. It's a job that resonates with Mooney because his entire career turned on a loan move, to Watford, in March 1994. He spent the next seven years at Vicarage Road.

* * *

Mooney was released by his home-town club, Middlesbrough, when he was a teenager. They decided not to offer him a youth training scheme contract, so he went to college, thinking his dream of being a professional footballer was over.

'I wanted to be an accountant but that was a four-year course, whereas book-keeping was three years,' he says. 'So I thought I'd do book-keeping because I'd get wages a year sooner. I thought I could do my accountancy qualification later.' But 14 months into his college course, Aston Villa

offered him a trial. That one-week trial turned into a one-year
training-scheme contract, then he was offered pro terms.

Here's the first of those little coincidences that tie Mooney
to Watford. The first-team manager at Aston Villa at the time
was Graham Taylor. And here's the second coincidence: 'The
day I signed my first professional contract, I played at Vicarage
Road for Aston Villa in the FA Youth Cup. We lost but the
thing I remember most about that day was that as the team bus
pulled up at the top of the steps in Occupation Road, the kit
man made sure I didn't have to carry the skip because I was
now a pro. Two of the youth training scheme lads carried it.
We lost but at least I didn't have to carry the skip, so that was
progress. I didn't know it then but years later I would walk down
those steps every day into the old stand at Vicarage Road.'

Youth Team

Tuesday, November 21st, 1989
FA Youth Cup, Second Round
Watford 2 Aston Villa 1
Half-time: 0—0
Scorers: Watford: Price, Rice; **Aston
Villa:** Elliot.
Watford: Sheppard, Evans, Fuller,
Price, Towler, Alsford, Bazeley, Har-
rison, Gallen, Meara, Inglethorpe.
Subs: Rice for Alsford, Proctor (not
used).
Aston Villa: Livingstone, Crisp, Bulli-
vant, Liddle, Smith, Elliot, Williams,
Mooney, Curruthers, Froggatt, Small.
Subs: Morgan, Walker (neither used).

By the summer of 1990, Mooney was 19 and a regular
goalscorer for the reserves. He was still raw but was recognised
as a hard worker with an eye for goal. The problem was, Aston
Villa had just finished runners-up to Liverpool in the league
and the likelihood of breaking into the first team was slim.

At the end of the season, all the young players sat outside

the manager's office waiting to be called in one by one. If a player came out smiling, it meant he'd been offered a contract. If he didn't, he'd been released.

'I came out smiling, so the lads thought I'd got a contract, but that wasn't actually the case,' says Mooney.

This is what happened. Mooney went in and Taylor said: 'We're not going to give you a contract but you have done well and you could have a career if you start lower down. You've scored goals in the reserves and you were borderline. I'm going to let you go on a free transfer but, to say thank you, you're going on holiday to Magaluf tomorrow with the first team.'

'That was typical GT,' says Mooney. 'I'm sacking you, but you're going to Magaluf for a holiday with the first team. Brilliant. The lads looked after me all week and I had a great time.'

Mooney found a place at Scarborough, in the bottom division of the league, and he established himself as a centre forward, scoring 30 goals in 129 games. The old wheeler-dealer Barry Fry took him to Southend, who were in Division One (now the Championship) for £100,000. Mooney was an instant hit, scoring five in his first ten games for the Shrimpers before Fry moved to Birmingham and Peter Taylor replaced him. Mooney soon found he was not Taylor's cup of tea.

'I was flying until Peter Taylor came in, and then I didn't play for four months,' he says. 'He got a lad in from non-league, who lasted less than a year in league football, and I was in the reserves. It was a really difficult time for me because I'd moved away from home for the first time, bought my first house, in Essex, and I wasn't playing. Then he stopped me going on loan to Middlesbrough a couple of times, which would have been a dream move. He didn't want me going on loan because he wanted to make the club's money back on me, but who was going to spend £100,000 on a player who was in the reserves?'

Here's another coincidence. The season before joining

Southend, Mooney had played for Scarborough against
Gillingham and came up against a veteran centre half who
looked anything but the stereotypical lower-division brute but
could dish it out nonetheless. The defender was tall, slender,
upright and angular but he read the game better than most, and
appearances could be deceptive.

'In the first half, he absolutely smashed me,' says Mooney,
almost wincing at the memory. 'I was doubled over in pain but
I refused to go down because I didn't want him to know he'd
hurt me, so I gave him a mouthful of abuse instead.'

That centre half was Glenn Roeder, who was to leave Gillingham, where he was player-manager, to take over at Watford.

'On the day I signed for Watford, Glenn reminded me of
the incident. He said: "You probably don't remember this..." I
interrupted and said: "I know exactly what you're going to say.
I do remember."

'He said: "Do you remember what you said to me?" I
repeated what I'd said that day, which was full of expletives, and
Glenn told me that he had realised at that moment that I wasn't
some young pushover. That was when I got on his radar and I
was lucky Glenn had a long memory because otherwise I might
not have got a move away from Southend.'

April 16, 1994
Watford 3 Southend United 0

By March, Watford were in danger of going down and
even Jack Petchey, who had held a wiry old grip on the
club's piggybank, realised that reinforcements were
necessary. In the space of a few weeks, Roeder brought
in Craig Ramage, Colin Foster and Keith Millen, plus a
couple of strikers on loan, Dennis Bailey and Mooney.

It was Bailey who made the most dramatic impact,
coming off the bench – replacing Mooney – to score

a late winner in an incredible 4-3 win at Peterborough United. But it was Mooney who quickly established himself as a crowd favourite.

It wouldn't happen these days, but back then there was nothing to stop a loan player facing his 'parent' club if neither objected and so, when Southend visited Vicarage Road in the final month of the season, Mooney knew he would have the chance to face his team-mates and the manager who didn't rate him. Inevitably, he scored.

'I have never gritted my teeth more in my whole life than in that moment,' he says. 'It took all my willpower not to go over to their bench and scream in the Southend manager's direction. Before the game, my dad had warned me not to do it. Fortunately, I had a couple of players on my back so I wasn't going to make it over there but I wanted to. I got a little wink off Glenn because he knew how low I'd been when I arrived.'

May 8, 1994
Crystal Palace 0 Watford 2

There was a celebratory atmosphere at Selhurst Park on the final day of the season but Watford did their best to play the role of party poopers. Palace had been promoted as champions.

'That was the biggest game I'd played in at the time,' Mooney says. 'Palace got presented with the trophy, it was a full house and it was on TV. They do a party well at Selhurst Park, although I could never have played for them. I scored a goal, and I do wonder if that helped secure a permanent move. We knew Furs [Paul Furlong] was going but I'd scored only once during my loan spell. Even after that one, it was only two in ten games but I think it was my all-round play that persuaded Glenn to sign me. I had been thinking about giving up the game and going back up north to play non-league. If I hadn't been on a decent contract at Southend, I'd have walked. The permanent transfer dragged on over the summer because Southend were asking silly money for me but in the end they got back what they paid for me.

'That started off my career again and I was part of the little travelling club coming round the M25 every day. Milly [Keith Millen] would start off in Croydon and pick Hessy [Andy Hessenthaler] up from Kent, then they'd get Colin Foster in Essex and me at Brentwood services. The worst seat to get was to be in the back behind Fozzy [Foster] because he was so tall and he pushed the seat right back. I used to volunteer to drive so I could get a comfortable seat. It wasn't so good when the M25 was bad but those hours in the car really helped team spirit. We had a great little group.'

Glenn Roeder had hoped to pair Mooney with Jamie Moralee, who he signed from Millwall during the summer of 1994. At £450,000, Moralee was Watford's most expensive signing since Gary Penrice in 1989, and the price-tag raised expectations. Unfortunately, Moralee was not a prolific striker and he was slow off the mark, and only scored four goals all season. Mooney only scored three (although he missed much of the second half of the season with a knee injury) but he made up for the lack of goals with his all-action play, and had the bonus of not being saddled with a large same transfer fee like Moralee.

'He was a really good guy, Jamie,' says Mooney. 'He was a typical Cockney wide boy. He had all the clothes and he knew this celebrity and that celebrity. He was the complete opposite to me but we really got on well, and on the training pitch we really hit it off. We just couldn't do it in matches because we were too similar.'

Moralee scored his first goal in a 4-2 derby defeat to Luton in mid-September. 'He got a lot of stick but he would never admit it if that was getting to him. He had this attitude of, "Nothing bothers me," but I think it did hurt him that he wasn't scoring goals. I put one on a plate for him against Luton and there was such a look of relief on his face. I was delighted for him and I thought he might get on a little run of goals but it never happened for him.

'The thing was, neither of us were quick and we both wanted to win the first ball. He wasn't the nippy little striker getting the knockdowns. It just never worked for him but the lads loved him because we could go to Langans for lunch whenever we wanted,' says Mooney.

January 6, 1996
Watford 1 Wimbledon 1

By the time the FA Cup third round came around the following season, Roeder's Watford were in decline. The tight, difficult-to-beat unit Roeder had steered to the fringes of the play-offs was hit by a string of injuries and the team was threatened by relegation.

Watford held Premier League Wimbledon to a draw at Vicarage Road but it was Mooney's goal that prompted an unusual celebration that made it onto the BBC comedy sports quiz They Think It's All Over.

The celebration had the Watford players lying on their backs waving their hands and feet in the air, like upturned beetles unable to get the right way up. The idea was born at the players' Christmas do in Kudos a couple of weeks earlier.

'One of the lads fell over on the dance floor,' says Mooney. 'I think it was Johnno [Richard Johnson]. He was like a machine on a night out. He could fall over, get back up and carry on going. Anyway, before the Wimbledon game we joked that we'd do that as a celebration if we scored.

'I hit a decent strike from the edge of the box and I remember thinking, "That'll look good on Match of the Day." As we were running back, Johnno reminded me: "Dead ants!" I knew we were going to look stupid but we did it anyway.

'While we were lying there, I could see Wimbledon's striker Mick Harford, who was a hard bloke, walking straight for us. There was no way he was going to go round us, and he ended up treading all over Kevin Phillips' chest.

'Because of the celebration the film crew got in touch and wanted to know what it was all about, so I said, fine, as long as they made a donation to the players' pool. The thing was, I realised that I couldn't tell the real story. I couldn't say it was because the lads got hammered in a nightclub at the Christmas do and someone fell over because we didn't want to come across as the typical drunken footballers. We weren't like that. We did have a great social group but we only went out on a night when we were off the next day. We used to go into St Albans and get a table at Harry Smith's, and at the next table there would be the Arsenal lads and they'd be drinking twice as much as us.

'Anyway, the guy who was doing the filming for the TV company had glasses that were so thick I could almost see inside the back of his head, so that started me giggling, and once I started I couldn't stop. In the end, I had to swear to make him stop the camera because I thought they couldn't show this on TV.

'When the programme went out, they showed about eight takes of me laughing and failing to tell this story, which was a fib anyway – I had to say it had been for a bet or something but it wasn't very convincing – and the lads absolutely hammered me for it.'

With relegation on the cards in the spring of 1996, Watford sent for Graham Taylor, and Mooney was reunited with the manager who had released him as a young professional at Aston Villa. 'I did wonder what would happen,' says Mooney. 'How much would he know about me? Would he want me? I was one of the big fish at Watford but that doesn't matter to GT.'

On his first day back at the club, Taylor called a meeting for all the players in the old press room under the main stand. 'He gave us all a piece of paper and a pen, and a few of the lads were looking at each other thinking, "Hold on – what's going on here?" We sat down and he sat at the front like he was the schoolteacher and we were the class doing a test. And that is exactly what it was – a test. I knew him. Every day was a test with GT. He asked us to all pick our team and he said it was up to us if we wanted to put our name on the top of the piece of paper so he could see who picked who.

'I've never had a manager come in on his first day and ask the players to pick the team. Whatever teams we picked wouldn't have made any difference to GT's selection but he was sounding us all out. Who would put themselves in the team? Who else would they pick? What shape would they play? But more than that, who had the strength of character to put their name on top of the piece of paper and possibly have to stand by their team in front of their team-mates, and who wanted to put it in anonymously?

'So, I put my name at the top of the page in capital letters, picked my team, put myself in it, drew a circle round my name and wrote underneath that "Captain". Partly it was a bit of banter but partly it was to show the gaffer that I could be counted on. Later on I knew I'd passed that test.

'Nothing ever happened at that football club without the gaffer having planned it. We had meetings about meetings but I don't mean that in a negative way. Nothing was left to chance. He knew everything that was going on and he took control of everything, whether it was ordering the tea bags for the canteen or signing the centre forward.

'The bloke is a genius. Without GT, there's many players like me who wouldn't have won what we won, wouldn't have the medals we've got and wouldn't have got the contracts we got. We argued about things at the time, and sometimes it felt like he was paying the contracts out of his own pocket, but that was his football club. It still is.'

But not even Graham Taylor could halt the slide into the third tier at the end of the 1995-96 season. Mooney scored three goals during the run-in, including a couple that earned a 3-3 draw against the champions-to-be, Sunderland. But it was not enough. Although he won the player of the season award, Mooney does not remember much about that season.

That summer, Taylor moved 'upstairs', taking on a general manager's role and Kenny Jackett was charged with the job of getting Watford back to the second tier at the first attempt. Although Watford were in contention for a play-off place for much of the season, they faded at the end. 'There were two many draws,' says Mooney of a campaign that saw Watford held to a stalemate in 19 of their 46 league games. There was even a four-month run that stretched from October 12 to February 22 during which Watford won three league games and drew 13. 'The expectations, going down into that division, were that it would be easy, but it wasn't easy at all,' says Mooney. 'We were going to poor grounds, playing on poor pitches in front of poor crowds, and everyone wanted to beat us. We're not the biggest club to have ever been down there but, at that time, we were the team everyone wanted to beat.

'Because we didn't have GT as the manager, but he was still at the club, it was tough. Kenny is a fantastic coach and he was then. He has a way of emphasising just the right part of every sentence he speaks to get his message across, and his eye for detail was fantastic, but if the players are honest, we were probably looking over Kenny's shoulder a bit, wondering when GT would be coming back in.

'At the end of the season, Kenny became a coach and GT was back as the manager. I am sure Kenny would look back at that year and say he learned more in one season than at any other time of his career, and I think he became an even better coach as a result of that experience. But having GT back on the bench, running the team, the pressure was on because he could not accept failure. He wanted to get promoted straight away and he made it clear to us what he expected.'

In May 1997, the players knew Taylor would be swapping the blazer and tie for a tracksuit, metaphorically-speaking, for the following season. Before they broke up for summer, there was a testimonial game for the groundsman Les Simmons against Arsenal, and Taylor was back in the dressing room.

'It was about half an hour before the game, and we were already changed when the gaffer says to me: "I've been thinking about it for a few weeks and I want you to play at centre-half."

'I thought he was joking. "You what?"

'He said he wanted me to play on the left side of three centre backs and I said: "Was there any chance you were going to tell me about it?" He said: "I'm telling you now. Don't worry, it's only a friendly." Then, as he turned away, he said: "Oh yes, they've got a kid up front called Nicolas Anelka who is lightning quick." I thought to myself: "Dear me, here we go." He was so quick. He gave me five yards head-start over ten yards and he still beat me by two. I wasn't sure it was the position for me but he kept picking me there when we came back for pre-season and I played there. To be fair, I wasn't a real centre half – I had Pagey [Robert Page] and Milly [Keith Millen] alongside me who were proper defenders – but I loved it. It was different. My job was to come out with the ball and hit the diagonal up to the front players. It wasn't rocket science to work out what to do with GT. I did my defending, covered well, tackled, swept up a bit and then played the ball up to big Jason Lee.'

February 28, 1998
Watford 3 Bristol Rovers 2

Taylor assembled a team that was not outside the top two places all season, although there was a mini wobble in the spring. Watford raced into a 2-0 lead but Bristol Rovers dragged themselves back into the match.

'I gave away the penalty for their equaliser near the end of the game,' says Mooney. 'It was a real centre forward's challenge – a sloppy, lazy tackle – and I felt I owed the lads one because this was a game we should have had wrapped up.'

With time running out, Mooney refused to give up.

'That goal sums me up,' he says. 'I was just stubborn. If we needed a goal, I used to push up, and there were only a couple of minutes left when I got the ball on the edge of their area and just ran at them. The defender tried to stop me, and I was down on one knee, but I got up and just kept going. Then I got a little half-turn and got it onto my left foot and just fired it into the corner.'

Mooney carried on running as the fans behind the goal at the Vicarage Road end surged down towards him. 'I had half the team on my back and the fans were grabbing me,' he says. 'As the fans rushed forwards, the advertising board tipped over and dragged all the way down my shin. I needed a couple of stitches later on, but who cares? We'd won the game. It wasn't the greatest of goals but it meant a lot because it kept us top of the table.

'I got the old video of the goals at the end of the season and I'll never forget Mike Vince's commentary: "Cometh the hour, cometh the man." A load of my mates got T-shirts printed up with that on the front.'

Watford went on to win the Second Division championship by beating Fulham at Craven Cottage on the final day of the season. 'It was my first ever promotion, my first medal, and I remember sitting in the pub after the game with the medal round my neck and a cigar. I didn't even like cigars, or Champagne, but that night I had both because I thought that was what you did. It had been a lovely sunny day, and I remember seeing Robbo [Paul Robinson] being carried around on the fans' shoulders and seeing how happy Big Jase [Jason Lee], my old mate from Southend, was. It was a great, great day because we had worked really hard and we deserved it.'

But after the summer, Mooney's position in the team was no longer guaranteed. Taylor signed an experienced, conventional centre half, Dean Yates, and he switched to a flat back four, which meant Mooney's place on the left side of three central defenders no longer existed. He was behind Robert Page, Keith Millen, Steve Palmer and Yates in the pecking order at the back, and was not much closer to the starting eleven in his old position either.

'I was unused sub a lot, and when I did come on, sometimes it was at centre half, sometimes it was up front,' he says. 'I didn't feel like I had a place anymore. What was I? I wasn't really a defender but if people saw me as a striker, I was a striker who'd hardly scored. I think I had one goal by Christmas. Anyone looking at my record would think, "No thanks."'

In fact, Mooney's first goal of the season was in a 1-1 draw at Huddersfield in mid-February. And yet, by the end of May, Mooney's place in Vicarage Road folklore was secure.

'That was the strangest season any footballer can have,' he says. 'I can't tell you how close I was to leaving. I felt like I'd wasted six months of my career. I'd played at the back for a season and done quite well but now I was just drifting and, as the weeks went on, I was getting lower and lower.

'I came on as sub at Ipswich and scored with a header from a corner. Instead of celebrating, I ran back to the halfway line and, with the angriest face I've got, I looked right over at GT and he was so not bothered. He didn't blink. I thought: "I'm going to have to go."

'Alex McLeish at Hibernian was interested and I think a fee was agreed, and I knew what wages they were offering, but GT said no.'

The defining game of Watford's season and, arguably, Mooney's career was against Tranmere Rovers on April 3. Allan Smart and Richard Johnson got sent off but Watford battled to a 2-1 victory that prevented the door from slamming shut on their rapidly-fading play-off hopes. Two days later, on Easter Monday, Watford rose again, at St Andrew's, and Taylor put Mooney in the starting line-up, as a striker, with another former Aston Villa man, Tony Daley, on the wing.

'That was great for me, because I knew Daley was going to get all the stick off the fans rather than me,' he says with a smile. 'And the game worked out perfectly because he set one up for me and I set one up for him and we won 2-1. It was the perfect scenario.'

Mooney had no idea he was about to embark on the hottest scoring streak of his career. Over the next 28 days, Mooney scored seven of Watford's 11 goals in a six-match run that yielded 16 points from a possible 18. A play-off place that looked as if it had slipped away was suddenly within reach.

'Before the Tranmere game, the manager gave us this speech, which was kind of his last roll of the dice, I think. He said we had eight games to go and that if we won seven of them we'd be in the play-offs, and the team that finishes sixth wins the final and goes up,' says Mooney. 'The manager brought in a sports psychologist, Ciaran Cosgrave, the guy in the pink shirt, and he was brilliant for us. We bought into what he was selling because we wanted to be a success. We stopped going to the pub, we trained every day and we kept winning.'

Mooney remembers the goals clearly. Against Birmingham: 'Kevin Poole was rushing out and I knew there was a chance he was going to smash my face in, but I still went for it and I scored. Watching it back afterwards I realised how much that would have hurt if he'd caught me.' Against Bolton: 'I missed a penalty but I was starting to play like there was nothing to lose, and when I had a chance to score with my head later, I took it. GT was always very complimentary about my heading ability because I could jump better than most people my size. Was GT being complimentary about my heading or derogatory about my feet? It depended which side of bed I got out of but when he mentioned about my heading ability it made me feel ten feet tall.' Against Crewe: 'Guy Whittingham rolled one through to me, I got it on my left foot and just smashed it in at the far post. It's not rocket science. If I got a chance, I wanted to shoot. I'd barely scored for two years and I think I was so low mentally that I just wanted to get my buzz back. I scored six months' worth of goals in a month.' Against Crystal Palace: 'I was on a roll by now and I felt like I was going to score in every game.'

April 27, 1998
Port Vale 1 Watford 2

'The match at Port Vale was the one for me,' Mooney says. 'That was when I started to believe. I'd scored four in four and I was thinking about getting five in five but I ended the night with six in five. By now, Michel Ngonge and I had a bit of an understanding growing. He was brilliant – either he'd flick it on and I'd run onto it, or it would be the other way around. We just clicked that night.

'I remember the light that night. The sun took an age to go down and when it finally was going down it shone through a big gap in the back of the stand. Then the floodlights went on, but they were horrendous, so it was like playing in the dark.

'After we won that match, I just knew. Getting on the coach, I think we all knew but we didn't dare say anything. I wanted to say, "Are you thinking what I'm thinking?" but I didn't want GT to hear me because he'd have gone mad. But there was this feeling on the bus that we were going to get promoted. I tell you, that is an amazing thing when everybody feels the same.'

May 1, 1998
Barnsley 2 Watford 2

'As much as the Port Vale goals were important, it was the one at Barnsley that means as much to me. It was a red-hot day in Barnsley and I don't think they've had a sunny day there since. I had a good chance in the first half that I missed but after the month I'd had I said,

"Let it go," because I knew I wouldn't miss two good chances. As it happened, it was the scrappiest goal of my life. It put us 2-1 up and it went off the back of my shoulder. There was a little melee in the middle of the goal, someone's shot got blocked and I just threw myself at the rebound, turned my back on it and it hit me on the shoulder and went in. The Watford fans were behind the goal and I ran around the post and, as I looked up, I saw my dad and my brother-in-law right there in front of me. My brother-in-law had lifted my dad up so he looked about 20 feet tall. To look up and see them there was brilliant – an outstanding memory.'

Although it doesn't officially count as one of Mooney's goals for Watford, there can be few more important strikes than his penalty in the shoot-out at the end of the play-off semi-final second leg at St Andrew's.

Watford led 1-0, thanks to Michel Ngonge's goal at Vicarage Road, but after two minutes of the second leg, Birmingham City levelled the tie.

'That second leg was probably a game too far for us,' says Mooney. 'We hadn't really played that well in the last league game against Grimsby but we'd done enough to win 1-0 and get into the play-offs. The first game against Birmingham was very tight and Michel had done really well to get the only goal. But at St Andrew's we didn't play at all. We just weathered the storm – that's all we did.

'The noise in the stadium was incredible. The atmosphere that night is why I signed for Birmingham later in my career. When Dele Adebola – who went on to be a team-mate of mine – scored after a couple of minutes, I've never experienced anything like it. That was the noisiest football match I've ever been at. I was screaming at the top of my voice to Michel and

Pete Kennedy, who were only 20 yards away, and I couldn't even hear my own voice.

'We defended well enough to avoid conceding a second goal but it was like all the nervous energy and adrenaline that had got us into the play-offs had left our bodies – until extra-time, that is. I'd had a bang-average game but I knew I was going to be number five in the shoot-out, which is arguably the most important one. It can be the winner, or it can be the one you have to score to stay in the competition.

'Kenny Jackett had called Furs' [Paul Furlong] penalty. He knew he was going to put it that way, and Alec saved it. Then Steve Palmer scuffed his. Alon Hazan's was perfect and he did that little dance afterwards. Our penalties were well struck but they were close. We had a couple go in off the bar.

'Walking up to take it was the scary bit. There were 30,000 Brummies booing me. It's the most scared I've ever been in my whole life, except for when my kids were born. When I watch it back, I can see the tension on my face. In fact, just talking about it now is causing me a little bit of angst.

'I hadn't allowed my family to come to the game. I didn't want them there in case it went tits up, so they were watching at home in a pub. I'd promised them they could come to Wembley but I didn't want them at Birmingham if we missed out. But that's the most pressure I've felt in a game of football.

'I put the ball down and I had only one thing in my mind. I was aiming to go straight through his [goalkeeper] eyes. If he'd stayed in the way, I'd have knocked his head off – I struck it that well. I've never hit a better one.

'When Chrissy Holland had his penalty saved by Alec, all I could think about was that I was going to play at Wembley. That's the dream of every schoolboy footballer in Britain, isn't it? The celebrations are a bit of a blur but there was one thing the lads wouldn't let me forget. In a live TV interview, I said:

"Mum, I'll get you a new dress for Wembley." They hammered me for that! But all I could think about was that my dad and my mum were going to watch me at Wembley.'

* * *

The build-up to Wembley felt like it lasted an eternity. There were ten long days to wait between the semi-final and the final at Wembley. 'The gaffer ask me and Milly [Keith Millen] to organise the suits, so we went to Ciro Citterio in the Harlequin and picked them, and made sure we looked good,' says Mooney. 'The day was the best of my professional life, although the game itself was poor. If Eidur Gudjohnsen had been the striker then that he later became, we could have been 3-0 down before half-time but then Wrighty [Nick Wright] scored that goal. I had a half-chance with a header in the second half but it wasn't my best game. It doesn't matter because we won the game. Smarty [Allan Smart] scored the second one right at the end and I can remember the relief knowing that nothing could go wrong now. What a finish that was, by the way. The outside of the boot in the last minute at Wembley? Who does that? He was one of the best finishers I ever played with but maybe he didn't have the confidence in himself that I had in him because he was excellent.

'At the end, I spent a good 20 minutes on the pitch, but it's impossible to soak it all in. I know GT went and stood on the halfway line and just looked at the end with all our fans in, celebrating, and I wish I'd done that. I wish I had that memory.

'I put a bit of grass in my sock but by the time I'd got back to the dressing room I'd forgotten about it, although I did pinch my hook from the dressing room. I took a screwdriver with me. I'd planned in advance – don't you worry about that! I knew they were pulling it down eventually so they wouldn't miss it! I got 'my' peg from the Wembley dressing room and it's in a box in my dad's loft now.

'I sat in the bath on my own with my boots on, with a can of beer, thinking that when all the lads came in, I'd go up and give my medal to my dad. And then we went to Sopwell House afterwards and GT paid for bacon sandwiches for everyone at five in the morning. What more could you ask for?

'It gives me a tear, thinking about Wembley. It still does.'

August 14, 1999
Liverpool 0 Watford 1

'We really thought we could win against Wimbledon in the opening game, but we lost,' says Mooney. 'Then we went up to Sunderland and Kev Phillips was always going to score against us, wasn't he? Then we had Liverpool away. That was when we realised what the Premier League was all about.

'We went up on the train, and as we walked out of the station to the team coach, there was a queue of taxi drivers and one of them spotted us in our Watford tracksuits and said in a broad Scouse accent: "Like lambs to the slaughter…"

'It was an amazing game because we had all kinds of weather. It was bright, hot sunshine at the start. I scored from a set-piece. Mark Williams and Robert Page both went for the same ball and it broke to me, and I scuffed it in from six yards. I was shouting, "I've scored at the Kop end." Whenever I see him, Pagey tells me I said it half a dozen times but I'm not sure I did. After that, there was a really heavy storm and I remember saying to the ref: "Don't you dare call this off, because if my goal doesn't count, I know where you live."

'We were hanging on at times but we did it, and I remember coming off the pitch and all I could think of was that taxi driver. I'd played in every division and I must admit I'd thought to myself before the season started: "What if I don't score in the Premier League?" So to get my first goal, to win our first points, was special. I looked back at the Kop and the Liverpool fans were applauding us off. They didn't like us for beating them but they respected us, and that's a huge thing for a footballer.'

August 21, 1999
Watford 1 Bradford City 0

'This was my favourite goal of my entire career because we worked on that move in training. The deep diagonal ball came up and I could see Peter [Kennedy] making the run in behind me, and I headed it over my right shoulder, which is not the natural way for me to head it. It's easier to flick it over my left shoulder. But it went for him, I peeled away and went straight in the box. The cross came in and I caught it just right.

'In the space of a week, we'd had two 1-0 wins in the Premier League and I'd scored both goals. As a striker, that's the perfect scenario because you are the story. There'd been the hype of Anfield and then another 1-0 win, and we had six points on the board.

'I really thought that if we could turn in displays like that, we could stay up, but it didn't work out like that.'

Mooney's season in the Premier League was curtailed by a crude challenge from Chelsea's centre half Marcel Desailly during the game at Vicarage Road in September. Mooney was sent on as a substitute with Watford leading 1-0 and about to take a corner.

'As I went running into the box he tried to stick two fingers in my eyes,' he says. 'As the corner came in, I tried to get my retaliation in.

'Five minutes later, I was on the wing, trying to whip one into the middle from near the left-hand corner flag when he came in and straight-legged me. I whipped the ball in and he hit my knee cap. My immediate reaction was to try to get up and knock him out but when I jumped up, I was in too much pain so I went back down. It was so swollen I couldn't tell my kneecap was round here,' he says demonstrating how far the bone had been displaced.

'It was a horrible challenge but bad challenges can happen. I gave out a few hidings in my time but if I was wrong, I apologised. What hurt me was that he didn't apologise. Even now, when I see him on the television, I can't bring myself to watch him. But the flip side to that was that after the game, which we won, I came out of our dressing room on crutches. I was at the bottom of those stairs in the old main stand that I was talking about earlier. I had my kit bag over my shoulder and I was wondering how I was going to make it to the top. Gianfranco Zola was there, reading a John Grisham book – in English – and he took my bag off my shoulder and I said: "No, no, I'm fine," but he said: "Hey, Tommy, give me your bag," and he carried it to the top of the stairs and gave it to my missus. Now that is a gentleman.'

By the time Mooney was fit to play for the first team, Watford were as good as relegated and, in the meantime, he'd seen players come in who did not share the same ethos as those who had been promoted.

'I lost seven-and-a-half months of the Premier League season and my mates were struggling and there was nothing I could do to help them. We were a good group of lads competing against superstars. We signed Xavier Gravelaine around Christmas time but he came for the money, not to play football. That was a mistake by GT but what could he do? We were desperate. I was out, Smarty was out, Gifton was out.'

April 7, 2001
Watford 2 Crystal Palace 2

According to Tommy Mooney, his goal against the Eagles was his 20th of the season, although some sources, including watfordfcarchive.com do not credit it as such because they gave his goal against Sheffield United early in the season as an own goal.

But Mooney is adamant. 'Every striker wants to get to 20 goals and that one against Palace was special to me because it was my 20th of the season, definitely.'

After a blistering start, Watford's promotion challenge faded dramatically, then their play-off hopes slipped away, and Mooney's future was a big talking point because his contract was expiring.

Just before the transfer deadline, towards the end of March, Nottingham Forest made a good offer for him. 'David Platt was the Forest manager and I used to clean his boots when I was at Aston Villa, so it's funny how my career kept going in circles,' he says. 'They offered half a million quid, which was a great offer because I was on a Bosman and could leave at the end of the season for nothing. Jimmy Gilligan [former Watford player and coach] was a coach at Forest, so we'd had discussions but GT put his foot down and said no because he believed we still had an outside chance of promotion. Then he called me into the office and really screamed at me – he bawled me out for speaking to another club when I shouldn't. I said that they had called me, not the other way round, but the way he saw it, I shouldn't have spoken to them because it was disrespectful.'

With a month, Mooney was back in the manager's office for a one-to-one chat and this time it spelled the end of two Watford careers.

'I went into his office and we had a fantastic conversation that we'd never had before. He showed me more respect in that conversation than in all the time I'd known him – not that I mean he was disrespectful, at all. What I mean was that it was the first time we ever had a conversation on an equal footing. It was a man-to-man chat, rather than him being the boss and me being the player. I knew something was happening because we sat on the sofa instead of at his desk with him on a slightly higher chair, which was the usual thing.

'I was still talking to Watford about a new contract. We'd seen a house in Harpenden that we wanted and I knew what I needed to earn to be able to get it. The thing was, my kids were little and I wanted to put them in a school and be able to keep them there, so it would mean staying in Harpenden for the long term. Watford got three-quarters of the way to offering what I wanted and I was still thinking they might meet it.

'Graham told me he was going and he told me to prepare to leave as well. I started to say that I'd see who the new guy was and that he might want me to stay but GT said: "No, you're going too." Then he explained that the guy who was coming in had given the club a list of the squad with ticks and crosses against each name and there was a cross against my name. I didn't know then that it was Gianluca Vialli. Graham didn't tell me that but he said: "Get ready to leave. You've had a great time, you've done really well but now you can go on and make a lot of money and be a success." I didn't realise it at the time but what Graham meant was that the 'Watford way' was going and that it was going to be different. Later on, I got the impression that the new manager might have been uneasy about the way supporters felt about me and that if he left me out it might cause issues, so they wanted to make it clear that I was going before they announced who the new manager was.

'In my mind, Graham Taylor should have been allowed to choose who went in after him. I think he had earned that right. It was tinged with sadness that I was leaving because I'd been at the club seven years.

'I had an offer from Everton – their interest started when I scored against them in the FA Cup – but I turned them down and chose Birmingham. People might think that's strange but the money on offer was the same at both clubs. I knew I wasn't a Premier League player. I had scored 20 goals and I knew I was a very good Championship player. I'd been promoted twice and I knew I could go to Birmingham and have that feeling again. Also, me mam didn't want me to end up rooming with Gazza [Paul Gascoigne] on away trips. She thought he'd ruin me!'

* * *

Gaining promotion to the Premier League with Birmingham was good but it wasn't as special as his time at Watford. 'We were all established players, all paid very well, and it was business. It wasn't the fun I had at Watford,' Mooney says. 'I went to Swindon, Oxford and then Wycombe, which was lovely. But if I had to say where my heart was, it's Watford. I spent more time there than anywhere else and I was very fortunate to experience the success we had.

'When we got promoted, we had an open-top bus tour round the town, and I remember while we went off on the bus tour, Elton John's mum [Sheila Farebrother] offered to look after our twin girls, who were six months old. She said: "Leave them with me... You're my favourite player."

'What about that, eh? I was Elton's mum's favourite player. You can't say much more than that, can you?'

6

These days it is very rare for Watford to play friendly games except during the build-up to the regular season.

But as recently as the late Eighties the Hornets filled gaps in their schedule with challenge matches, testimonials and sometimes went on an overseas end-of-season tour before breaking up for summer.

This chapter looks at some of the more unusual games Watford played between 1979 and 1987. There were trips to China and the West Indies, matches that embraced the game's past and possible future, and the club's only clash with Barcelona. (So far, at least.)

How many do you remember?

THE FRIENDLY GAMES

Formed as Watford Rovers in 1881, it was five years before the club took part in a competitive fixture. Up to that point all the team's matches had been friendlies, with nothing at stake except local pride, but that changed when they faced Swindon Town in the FA Cup first round on Saturday, October 23, 1886. Watford lost that tie 1-0 but were regulars in the FA Cup and other knockout competitions from then on, although another decade passed before the club joined an organised league. In the meantime, there had been a merger and a name change and so, by the time the club was invited to join the Southern League Division Two shortly before the turn of the century, it was known as West Herts.

Friendlies continued to play a part, either as practice games for more important fixtures, or benefit matches for long-serving players or staff, or simply to raise much-needed cash.

In the 1950s, a pre-season custom was established where the Blues (a team playing in Watford's home colours) took on the Whites (wearing the away shirt). More often than not, these were matches between Watford's 'probables' – the players who were most likely to make the first team – and the 'possibles' – those who were challenging for a place in the starting line-up.

Later on that decade, Watford played host to a succession of foreign opponents, often in floodlit matches held on mid-week evenings. Floodlights were installed at Vicarage Road in 1953 and so evening kick-offs became popular with supporters, and the club, which could generate income between Saturday league games.

Hajduk Split from Yugoslavia (1-0 to Watford), FC Wien of Austria (1-0), Portuguesa des Desportos (2-5), Borussia Dortmund of West Germany (4-1) and Sturm Graz of Austria (1-1) all visited between 1954 and 1956. In April 1957, Glasgow Celtic came down from Scotland and won 4-0 in front of almost 10,000 supporters.

Throughout the 1960s and 1970s, friendlies involving Watford varied from warm-up games and testimonials against non-league outfits to the occasional match against more glamorous opposition, such as Arsenal (for George Catleugh's testimonial in 1964 and again for Ken Furphy in 1969) and the Great Britain Olympic team (several times at the end of the 1960s and early 1970s).

In more recent years, there have been some significant pre-season friendlies. The German striker Jurgen Klinsmann made his first appearance for Tottenham Hotspur in a 1-1 draw at Vicarage Road in August 1994. When Gianluca Vialli took over as manager in 2001, Watford played Internazionale in Lecco, and at Sampdoria, losing 2-1 and 4-0. Five years later, as Watford prepared for a season in the Premier League, Inter visited Watford and were held to a 1-1 draw. Since the Pozzo takeover, Watford have played the other two clubs in the family, beating Granada 2-0 in 2013 and drawing 2-2 with Udinese the following summer.

But this chapter looks at a period between 1979 to 1987 when Watford took part in a number of remarkable matches. Did you know, for example, that the Hornets provided the opposition for a team bound for the 1982 World Cup? Or that Watford once won the Great Wall of China Cup? Or do you remember the one and only time they played the mighty Barcelona? Read on, and find out more.

THE FRENCH CONNECTION
May 1979 – Sochaux 0 Watford 0

This tale says as much about Graham Taylor's ambition and sense of foresight as it does anything else.

In May 1979, Watford were battling to get out of the Third Division and were locked in a promotion race with Shrewsbury Town, Swindon Town and Swansea City. A victory over Sheffield Wednesday on May 5 put the Hornets top of the table with one game remaining but they knew they could still miss out if the teams below them won their games in hand.

Only victory against Hull City on May 14 could ensure promotion but while Taylor was concentrating on leading the club out of the lower divisions, he also saw an opportunity to practise for the future.

It seems unthinkable now that a team with such an important game ahead of them would head off to France to play a friendly but that is what they did. The squad travelled to north-eastern France to play against French First Division side Sochaux three days before the showdown against Hull.

Months earlier, Watford and Sochaux had agreed to play a couple of friendlies: one in France and then a return match at Vicarage Road later in the year. The first game was played on a training ground at the headquarters of Adidas France in Landersheim, not far from Sochaux's base in Montbéliard.

With a sense of foresight that some might have considered presumptuous, Taylor decided to treat the games as if they were the two legs of a European tie. His plan was to go to France and play for a nil-nil draw and then win the 'tie' at home.

As Taylor says: 'I told the players to imagine we'd been drawn away from home first and we needed to get a goalless draw to bring back to Vicarage Road. I never sent a team out onto the pitch aiming for anything less than a win, so in that respect it was unusual.'

Taylor selected a defensive line-up with four at the back and another of his central defenders, Ian Bolton, alongside Dennis Booth in a deep midfield position. The phrase 'holding mid-fielder' wasn't used then but that's what Bolton and Booth were that day.

Already known for their direct, attacking style, Watford employed alien techniques to waste time. Their play was so tedious that Steve Sherwood spent much of his time dribbling the ball across the edge of his penalty area and back. In those days, the goalkeeper could pick the ball up from a backpass and so he'd roll it out to one full-back, collect it back, pick it up, dribble across his box and roll it out to the other full-back.

'I asked them to be defensively-minded and to play not just for a draw but for a nil-nil draw,' says Taylor. 'It was an experiment but I was interested to see how the players coped with the instruction. We spent a lot of time passing from the goalkeeper to the defenders and back again.'

'It was a very strange game,' says Bolton now. 'From memory, I think we played on an all-weather pitch, which made it very different to what we were used to. We were an all-action team, very aggressive, very attacking and to try to keep the ball under control and not look to get forward and attack was completely alien to us.'

Taylor remembers the players were not keen on the approach. 'A few of them said to me afterwards that they never wanted to play like that again,' he says.

Sochaux weren't happy either. In fact, they were downright offended and cancelled the 'return leg'.

'They refused to come to Vicarage Road later in the year and I don't blame them,' says Taylor. 'It was a bit naughty of me, really.'

'I don't blame 'em either,' says Bolton. 'They'd have got a right hammering at our place.'

A couple of days after boring Sochaux into submission in France, Watford returned to Vicarage Road and thumped Hull City 4-0 to confirm their place in Division Two.

And just over four years later, Watford experienced European competition for real when the qualified for the Uefa Cup, defeating Kaiserslautern from West Germany and Levski Spartak of Bulgaria before being knocked out by the slick Czech side Sparta Prague. In a couple of those matches, Ian Bolton was deployed not at centre half but as a holding midfielder, in front of the back four, just as he had been against Sochaux.

So the trip to north-eastern France wasn't entirely wasted.

RED STAR AT NIGHT
February 1981 – Watford 2 Red Star Belgrade 2

Less than a month before their European Cup quarter-final tie against the Italian giants Internazionale, Red Star Belgrade, the champions of Yugoslavia, visited Vicarage Road on a soggy night in March 1981.

Watford were a Second Division team and Red Star were among the most powerful teams in Europe, so why did they want to play the match?

The Yugoslav league had just finished its winter break and Red Star needed games to get back up to speed before the tie against Inter and so they headed for a short tour of England. They were due to face West Bromwich Albion and Nottingham Forest, and when Watford were offered the opportunity to host them, at short notice, they snapped up the offer because Graham Taylor was always keen to test his players and expose them to new challenges.

Taylor sent his coach Sam Ellis to watch Red Star against West Brom and Forest and reported back to say that they were a technically accomplished side packed with Yugoslav

internationals, including the captain Vladimir Petrovic. Before
the match, Taylor said: 'This sort of side could smack our
bottoms very soundly, and there is no way we would want that
if it can be avoided, so we are preparing for them.'

The Yugoslav players travelled to Vicarage Road to watch
the Hornets play out a dour 0-0 draw against Cambridge United a week before the two sides were due to meet. It is fair to say
the Yugoslavs were not unduly concerned. Their coach, Branko
Stankovic, said: 'The game was faster than we are used to, but
less thoughtful. No one seems to put their foot on the ball. It
is all action.'

The game itself was held in terrible conditions with wind,
rain and a heavy pitch making it difficult to appreciate the skills
of the Yugoslavs. Nevertheless, they took the lead in the first
half and doubled it early in the second before the match ignited
with a few strong challenges. Watford played Red Star at their
own game and joined in with niggling fouls and time-wasting
before an own goal got them back in the contest. Northern
Irish striker Gerry Armstrong equalised and Stankovic, the Red
Star coach, was impressed by Watford's stamina. 'Their physical
fitness told and our midfield collapsed in the second half.'

AN EVENING OF RAZZAMATAZZ
March 1981 – Watford 1 Vancouver Whitecaps 0

Long before Jay DeMerit played for the Vancouver Whitecaps,
Watford had an association with the Canadian club. Steve
Harrison, who went on to be a coach and then manager, joined
Watford from the Vancouver Whitecaps in 1978 and, although
it was not widely known at the time, Graham Taylor had been
approached to manage the Whitecaps in 1980.

Elton John even suggested he travel over to Canada to
speak to them, even though he had little intention of joining,
although that had more to do with the Whitecaps' offer of

first-class flights for him and his wife, Rita.

By 1981, North America was experiencing the tail-end of its first great love affair with soccer. The NASL had boomed in the 1970s, attracting Pele, Franz Beckenbauer and George Best but also a host of journeymen pros from the English leagues.

This was a land of opportunity and innovation – a place that introduced Astroturf, squad numbers and razzamatazz.

Ken Furphy, who had led Watford to the Second Division for the first time at the end of the 1960s, headed to the States to manage Pele and the New York Cosmos. Watford winger Stewart Scullion played for Tampa Bay Rowdies and Portland Timbers, while other former Hornets Colin Franks went to the Toronto Blizzards and Keith Eddy finished his career in the Big Apple with the Cosmos. Elton John even owned a stake in the Los Angeles Aztecs for a short time in the 1970s.

In the spring of 1981, Watford striker Ross Jenkins joined the Washington Diplomats, who were now managed by Furphy. In *Enjoy the Game*, Jenkins described the experience: 'America was a very strange place to play football,' he said. 'It was like being in The Jetsons. I'd been put in this team with ten other people and we were just trying to get some kind of understanding. You would get on a plane with them and take off and fly for hours over nothing much in particular, and then the plane would screech to a halt near some skyscrapers. You might be in Florida, or San Jose or Canada. You got off the plane and took a bus to a great big stadium with no one in it and you'd play on Astroturf or this crushed-up stuff like a clay tennis court, and then you'd get back on the plane and fly back to where you'd come from.'

Shortly after arriving in Washington, there was an assassination attempt on the president, Ronald Reagan, and Jenkins was kept inside at his motel when there was a long lock-down by police. 'Like I said, it was an experience,' he said.

Anyway, the Americans had not really taken to soccer. For a start they didn't understand the concept of playing a game and reaching the conclusion without a winner.

But American sports did lead the way in terms of commerce. They had comfortable all-seater stadia, more women and children attending, and sporting occasions were more of an event. English football in the early 1980s was in the doldrums. Hooliganism had led to the fans being caged in by fences, something that Watford were determined to avoid inflicting on their own supporters. Elton and the club's chief executive, Eddie Plumley, had travelled to the States a few times to see if they could take inspiration from their matchday experience.

In March 1981, the Vancouver Whitecaps arrived at Vicarage Road for an evening that borrowed some of the razzle dazzle. A troupe of drumming majorettes entertained the crowd before the players were called onto the pitch one by one.

The two teams agreed to ban the backpass to the goalkeeper for the night and the goalkeepers made a gentleman's agreement that they would kick it clear rather than pick it up if they received the ball from one of their own players. A klaxon sounded each time a defender passed back to his own goalkeeper.

The occasion was dampened by more terrible weather and had it been a reserve team game, they'd have cancelled it to save the muddy pitch further punishment.

Although Watford won 1-0, with a goal from Malcolm Poskett, the two teams staged a US-style shoot-out after the final whistle. This wasn't like a penalty shoot-out. Instead the players dribbled from the centre circle and had 30 seconds to beat the goalkeeper. Keith Pritchett and Ian Bolton scored Watford's goals in the 2-2 shoot-out draw. More than 10,000 supporters watched the game but it's fair to say the drumming majorettes failed to capture the imagination.

A TRIP DOWN UNDER
1982 – Australia and New Zealand

Watford had just won promotion to the top flight for the first time and were in the mood to party, so how better to celebrate than a trip Down Under?

A couple of days after the end of the season, the squad boarded the plane bound for Melbourne.

Ian Bolton doesn't remember much about the flight. 'Me and Roy Clare, the kit man who is now longer with us, sadly, sat down at the back of the plane with a deck of cards and a bottle of Jack Daniels. We played crib and both got legless. I missed the stop in Germany, missed the stop in India and the thing that woke us up was touching down in Melbourne.

'We arrived in the evening, went straight to bed, got up in the morning, trained, played a game in the evening and then flew straight to New Zealand, so I couldn't tell you what Australia was like.'

The first match on the tour was a 4-0 win over Victoria State in front of 7,000 fans in Melbourne but the main purpose of the trip was to play three games against the New Zealand team, who were about to head to Spain to play in the 1982 World Cup.

'We landed in New Zealand and we were greeted by these massive blokes in grass skirts, sticking their tongues out, eyes bulging,' says Bolton. 'I now know they were doing the traditional Haka, their war dance, but they were doing it in such an aggressive way. This guy was right in my face and I thought I was going to knock him out.

'The games were much more competitive than we'd been expecting. We'd just won promotion and were on cloud nine, looking forward to the First Division but also there for a jolly, a bit of a holiday, after a long, hard season. They were preparing for the World Cup and we were an English club side so perhaps they wanted to prove themselves because in the first game they tried to kick chunks out of us. That galvanised us as a group and we were determined not to get bullied.'

That first match, in Christchurch, ended in a narrow 1-0 win for Watford, thanks to a goal from John Barnes. The second match, in Wellington, was a keenly-fought 1-1 draw and Les Taylor felt the full force of the Kiwis early on. 'After about eight minutes, I went up for a header and I clashed heads with the guy I was challenging for the ball with. I landed on my feet and he landed in a heap on his back so I thought I'd come off okay but then I realised I had a bad gash under my eye. I ended up with 40 stitches around my eye. I had relatives over there and they'd come to see me but they only saw me play eight minutes.'

The final game in Auckland ended in a 2-0 win for Watford but Bolton remembers the trip more than the matches. 'We were a bunch of lads who'd come from the Fourth Division and now we were getting the chance to go on some amazing trips,' he says. 'The weather was nice. We had a great craic with all our fellow players and it felt like a reward for what we'd achieved. I absolutely loved New Zealand. It was like going back in time 30 years. We met the Prime Minister in Auckland and he had just walked to work through the park. Even then it felt like another world.'

CASUAL MEETING
March 1983 – Watford 6 Corinthian Casuals 1

Corinthian Casuals were one of the most famous amateur clubs in England and still adhered to some of the old amateur ethos. The club was officially formed in 1939, when two clubs from the leafy, already affluent Surrey countryside to the south-west of London, merged. Those two clubs, Corinthians and Casuals, were formed in 1882 and 1883, respectively, and so in 1982-83 the club, stalwarts of the non-league system, was marking the centenary of its roots.

It was quite a coup for the Casuals to secure a friendly against Watford, who were sitting second behind Liverpool in the First Division when they played the match at Vicarage Road on March 28, 1983. And they could hardly have asked for more fitting opponents because Watford fully embraced the sense of occasion.

This wasn't the first clash between the two sides. They had met in a friendly more than 50 years earlier, in 1932, when Tommy Barnett and Arthur Woodward were among the scorers in a 3-2 win in a friendly game. The Corinthians had pockets in their shorts and as Barnett recalled: 'The Corinthians didn't run out – they strolled out with their hands in their pockets.'

Watford asked their kit suppliers, Umbro, to produce some special shirts and so the players turned out in red, green and yellow-hooped rugby-style cotton shirts with button-up collars, baggy shorts and hooped socks. The shirts were replicas of one of the first kits Watford wore in the early 1900s.

Goalkeeper Steve Sherwood and physio Billy Hails both wore large flat caps and Graham Taylor went the whole hog on the touchline, donning a three-piece suit, bowler hat and stick-on moustache.

Taylor took things even further, sending his Watford team onto the pitch in the old W M formation with two full backs, three half backs and five forwards. Pat Rice, Steve Sims and Wilf Rostron were the defenders and, as Taylor said, the experiment served a purpose: 'At 38, I suppose I was in the last age group to play the old W and M formation at school,' said the manager. 'But it served as an exercise in what to do when we were outnumbered at the back.'

At the time, Watford frequently lined up with four forward players – John Barnes and Nigel Callaghan were old-fashioned wingers with Luther Blissett and, usually, Ross Jenkins, in the centre. Against Corinthian Casuals, there were five front men, with central defender Steve Terry as a battering ram-style centre forward.

Terry opened the scoring after 11 minutes and Worrell Sterling, Jan Lohman and Ian Richardson made it 4-0 before half-time.

At some point in the second half, Pat Rice pretended to get injured so that Billy Hails could run on and demonstrate the fabled 'magic sponge' approach to treatment. The stunt was arranged in advance but what Rice didn't know was that Hails was going to throw a full bucket of water in his face as a joke.

In the second half, David Johnson added a fifth before Graham Taylor came on as a substitute. It is the only time Taylor pulled on his boots to play in a proper match for Watford at Vicarage Road in front of a paying crowd. Speaking of which, Watford rolled back the years when it came to admission fees too. At the time it cost £2.50 to watch a First Division match from the terraces at Vicarage Road. That night, Watford charged 50p to stand and a pound for a seat.

In his 16 minutes on the pitch, Taylor watched as a header flew wide but his main contribution to the match, aside from wearing a fake moustache, of course, was to give away a penalty that Charlie Chaplin would have been proud of. As the clock ticked down, with Watford now leading 6-0 after Sterling scored his second, Taylor pushed one of the Casuals squarely in the back with both hands to give them a chance of getting on the scoresheet, which they took.

FROM JAMAICA TO CHINA
May 1983

The morning after beating champions Liverpool 2-1 at Vicarage Road to clinch second place in the league, Watford's players gathered at Heathrow airport for a 13-hour flight to Kingston, Jamaica. When they arrived, they were greeted like the Beatles. A huge crowd and several TV crews were there, mainly to see Jamaican-born Luther Blissett and John Barnes, who had become heroes after the Hornets had taken the First Division by storm.

Most of the trip was spent relaxing – sunbathing by the pool, water-skiing in the sea. Ian Bolton had a go at limbo-dancing and the players feasted on goat curry.

Toward the end of the trip, they played a game against a hastily assembled Team America, made up of players from the Caribbean and the United States. The game, played on a dusty, bone-hard pitch, was not a classic. It ended in a 1-1 draw but the 33,000 crowd was a record for a match played on the island at the time and Blissett's headed equaliser brought the house down.

After a few days back in England, the squad were on the move again, this time travelling with Elton John and the board of directors to China. Watford's tour to China had been months in the making and was planned as part of a British trade delegation to open up new business links with a booming industrial and economic power. For their part, the Chinese wanted to make football more popular so that they might one day compete in the World Cup. The trip was so momentous that the writer Martin Amis went along and wrote about his experiences for the *Observer*. His brilliant essay, Watford in China, also appears in the book *Visiting Mrs Nabakov and Other Excursions* and is well worth reading.

For many of the players, it was an eye-opener, not least because of the cuisine on offer. There were fish stomachs, pungent ancient eggs, things that looked like insects that turned out to be insects. The players immediately asked for steak and chips and their Chinese hosts did their best to accommodate.

The weather was oppressively hot and humid, and the games themselves were not particularly challenging as the standard of play from the Chinese national team and the Shanghai XI they faced was poor.

More than 80,000 people were inside the People's Stadium in Peking, as Beijing was commonly called then. It was the largest crowd a Watford team had ever played in front of.

'We arrived at the stadium and there were 80,000 bikes outside,' says Les Taylor. 'All the bikes were identical. I couldn't help wondering if people bothered to find their bike or just took any old one.'

Despite the huge crowd, the atmosphere was surreal. 'They were silent,' says Ian Bolton. 'The crowd didn't know the game and they were being taught how to cheer as the game went on. Sometimes they cheered the strangest things, like the ball going off for a throw-in.

'I definitely got a sense of being the outsider on that trip. China was closed to the rest of the outside world in those days and I wonder what they thought of seeing blond-haired people and black people. They must have thought we'd come from a different planet. I remember the first night when we sat down for dinner thinking, "Oooh, Chinese food, this'll be good." I had no idea. I was expecting a chow mein and a fried rice like we got from the take-away. It was very, very different.'

Elton went on a spending spree and the players went on excursions, including to the Great Wall, although according to Amis's essay, John Barnes skipped that particular day trip.

'We got on a coach and drove for three hours past nothing but countryside,' says Bolton. 'I think I might have had a hangover and there was a lot of mickey-taking and messing about. There was a touch of the school outing about it. We got there and it's a wall. But it's the only thing that can be seen from space and hundreds of people died building it, but at the time all I could think was, "We've driven three hours to see a wall." I was standing there thinking, "Is this it?" I was so ignorant about things at that time that I didn't appreciate it. I didn't really take everything in but, in hindsight, it was an amazing trip and an incredible opportunity, and I appreciate it now.'

Watford won the first game, against a Chinese National XI, 3-1, then travelled to Shanghai, where they won 2-1. The first game in Peking had been such a success that the Chinese officials were keen to arrange another game before Watford went home, so they faced the China team again and won 5-1 this time.

In between there had been another sightseeing trip, to the Yellow River. 'We went on a ferry,' says Les Taylor. 'They had put us in first class and it was just Elton and us players, and it was a bit boring because no one else was in there, so we went down to tourist class and it was full of Americans. We went and told Elton and he was straight down there, signing autographs and having a laugh with them.

'We went back to Peking and the London Ballet were staying in our hotel. We came back after our game and they'd just finished their performance. I can remember some of our players dancing with the ballet dancers. Steve Terry was holding one above his head.'

BARCELONA
August 1984 – Barcelona 2 Watford 1

The summer after the FA Cup final defeat to Everton in 1984, Graham Taylor went on holiday and left his assistant, John Ward, in charge, saying more or less: 'If anything happens, take care of it yourself.'

Ward got a call from Gerry Armstrong, who had left Watford the previous summer to join Real Mallorca in the Spanish league. Armstrong had a proposal – would Watford like to take part in a four-team tournament on the Balearic island with the hosts, Barcelona and Rapid Vienna of Austria?

This sounded like a great opportunity to spend a week preparing for the new season in the sunshine, play a couple of games against top quality opposition and all expenses were paid, so, after consulting with Bertie Mee, Ward accepted a trip out to Majorca to check out the hotel and training ground where Watford would be based. Impressed with the facilities on offer, Ward agreed to enter the tournament.

But, in typical Spanish mañana fashion, the level of organisation was not all that Ward had hoped. Instead of the exclusive retreat tucked away from the tourist traps that Ward had been shown, Watford were to be based near the nightspots – something that Taylor would have wanted to avoid given that some of his players (Maurice Johnston's name springs to mind here) would gravitate towards them like a moth to a flame.

Rapid Vienna had withdrawn from the competition and had been replaced by Universidad of Chile, and the two matches Watford were scheduled to play were on consecutive nights, kicking off at 10pm and 10.30pm because temperatures could still be stifling at 8pm.

'It turned out Barcelona were staying at the hotel I'd been shown,' said Ward. 'It was boiling hot during the day so we couldn't do the fitness sessions we needed to do. To put it bluntly, it had all gone wrong.'

Watford almost pulled out of the tournament but decided to go through with it when the organisers found them a more suitable hotel.

To add to all that, Watford's first game was also Terry Venables' first game in charge of Barcelona, bringing Graham Taylor face to face with his old nemesis again. Taylor and Venables had rubbed each other up the wrong way over the years as their teams, Watford and QPR, came face to face. Venables had complained about the slope on the pitch at Vicarage Road and Taylor's so-called 'long ball' tactics. Taylor had returned the volley with top-spin by criticising the plastic pitch at Loftus Road and QPR's reliance on the offside trap. Elton John had even joined it at one point, adding fuel to the flames by describing Venables as an East End barrow boy.

Now Venables had been dubbed El Tel but his first game in charge of one of the most famous clubs in European football was against a team that had always caused him problems.

Watford were short of defenders so Taylor opted for a continental-style formation, with Wilf Rostron deployed as a sweeper behind a back three of David Bardsley, Lee Sinnott and Kenny Jackett. Les Taylor sat deep in midfield with Nigel Callaghan and John Barnes taking wide positions and Luther Blissett playing just behind the front two of Maurice Johnston and George Reilly. That's a sweeper and a diamond-shaped midfield – a formation that at the time would have been seen as the height of continental sophistication.

The game didn't get off to the best start. In the first minute, Lee Sinnott slipped and handled the ball in the area and Barcelona's Bernd Schuster scored from the penalty spot. The West German midfielder was in his pomp at the time and made for a formidable opponent, as Les Taylor recalls. 'He was very difficult to pick up because he dropped deep to get the ball, played it and then popped up on the edge of our box without us really realising how he got there. He was always a step ahead and you could see his quality.'

Barcelona doubled their lead when Rojo scored but Maurice Johnston pulled one back with a header at the far post just before half-time. The second half was played at little more than walking pace and even as midnight approached it was still very hot and humid.

The following night Watford played Real Mallorca and again fell behind early on before Johnston equalised. The home team scored again to consign Watford to another 2-1 defeat and

Gerry Armstrong came on and played the last 20 minutes or so against his former club.

Although both games were friendlies and were played at less than competitive pace, that didn't mean they were for the faint-hearted. Both Barcelona and Real Mallorca knew every trick in the book and, as the man who had to lead Watford's attack, George Reilly bore the brunt of their aggression. During the Mallorca match, one of the defenders spat in his face and he remembers: 'It smelled of garlic – it was absolutely horrible – so I dropped him, just forearm-smashed him.'

Taylor substituted Reilly to save him from more punishment, or perhaps save him from himself.

With just a week to go before Watford were due to start their First Division campaign against Manchester United at Old Trafford, it was not the perfect preparation but Taylor had held his tongue. As Ward said in *Enjoy the Game*: 'I felt terrible because it was a disaster. The players hadn't kicked off about it, and fortunately no one knew I'd planned it.'

But as Taylor and Ward took their seats on the plane home, Taylor lent over and quietly said to his assistant: 'Well, Wardy, I don't think we'll be doing that again, will we?'

'It was so simple and it was the biggest put down I've ever had in my life but I had to respect him,' said Ward. 'I knew he'd hated every minute of that trip but he put up with it and he didn't give me a hard time because he knew he'd let me get on with things while he was away, and I'd just got it wrong. Other people would have made a fuss but that was the mark of the man.'

Unless Watford qualify for the Champions League, or the Pozzos issue an invitation to Barcelona to visit Vicarage Road for a pre-season friendly, Johnston's goal will remain the only one scored by a Hornet against the Catalan giants. Although Watford have faced Inter Milan twice since, Barcelona remain arguably the most famous opponents the club has faced.

A PUBLIC PRACTICE MATCH
FEBRUARY 1985 – Yellows 3 Whites 2

The weather was bad in February 1985, causing a run of post-ponements and leaving Watford without a game for two weeks.

So, the club announced that the Yellows would face the Whites at Vicarage Road on Saturday, February 16 and that entry would be free for anyone who wanted to watch.

Around 3,000 people turned up to see a game Watford couldn't possibly lose.

The yellows, wearing the team's home strip, were represented by Tony Coton, Lee Sinnott, Wilf Rostron, Steve Terry, John McClelland, Les Taylor, Jan Lohman, Worrell Sterling, Luther Blissett, George Reilly and John Barnes.

The whites, in the away kit, were Steve Sherwood, David Bardsley, Neil Price, Cliff Powell, Kenny Jackett, Alan Paris, Gary Porter, Nigel Callaghan, Malcolm Allen, Jimmy Gilligan and Paul Atkinson.

The Yellows had the firepower as they won 3-2 with goals from Worrell Sterling, Luther Blissett and John Barnes. Alan Paris and Malcolm Allen replied for the Whites.

MEETING THE BRAZILIAN CHAMPIONS
March 1987 – Sao Paulo 1 Watford 1

The morning after Watford had stunned Arsenal in the FA Cup quarter-final at Highbury in March 1987, the players were at Heathrow airport waiting for a flight to the West Indies. This was not a mid-season break from the hectic fixture schedule, or even a trip to the warm weather as a reward for reaching the FA Cup semi-final. Watford were scheduled to play Sao Paulo, the champions of Brazil, in an exhibition game in Trinidad.

John Barnes and Luther Blissett were still big draws in

the West Indies, which is why Watford were invited to play, although they only accepted on the basis that they would have to cancel if their cup tie against Arsenal went to a replay.

There was a minor problem with the British West Indies Airways plane on its inbound journey. After a long delay, the flight was cancelled and Watford's officials, who were reluctant to disappoint their hosts or forego the appearance fee for playing in Trinidad, set about making alternative arrangements.

In the end, they took a coach from Heathrow to Gatwick, where they checked into a hotel for the night before flying out to the Caribbean 30 hours later than planned.

That limited the amount of time the players had to relax, although they did find time to swim and sunbathe. Some went fishing and others watched an hour's cricket at the Trinidad Oval, during which time they saw eight wickets fall.

On a dry, dusty pitch the match wasn't much to look at, although Blissett scored a terrific equaliser in the 1-1 draw that sent a capacity 33,000 crowd into raptures. After the final whistle, the players had just 40 minutes to shower and change and get on the coach back to the airport for their flight home.

The team arrived at 9.30 on Thursday morning but were called into training on Friday morning to prepare for Saturday's league game, which was another clash with Arsenal.

'On the Friday, the manager had us playing a full eleven-a-side game, first team against reserves,' says Gary Porter. 'We were jet-lagged but he wanted us to run the jet-lag off. Malcolm Allen was playing centre forward for the reserves and he was running rings round McClelland. John wasn't stupid; he was a wily old fox, saving his legs for the following day, but Graham wasn't happy. He blew his whistle and said: "We'll be here until six o'clock unless you start putting some effort in."'

'Malcolm always caused me problems,' says McClelland now. He was a little player, with a low centre of gravity, and he could turn his hips and change direction very quickly. Some players just give you trouble.'

The following day, Watford beat Arsenal 2-0. In eight days, they had beaten the Gunners twice and flown halfway round the world to play against the Brazilian champions. All in a week's work.

THE RETURN TO CHINA
May 1987

Graham Taylor's final match in charge of Watford before he joined Aston Villa was a testimonial for long-serving goalkeeper Steve Sherwood against Heart of Midlothian at Vicarage Road on May 12, 1987. Earlier that afternoon, Watford's board of directors met at the ground and, at the end of the meeting, Taylor mentioned that he had been approached, informally, unofficially, by Villa. The reaction of the directors told him it was time to go. The story is told in full in *Enjoy the Game* but the short version is that Watford beat Hearts 4-3 in the evening and by the weekend Elton John had appointed Dave Bassett as Taylor's replacement.

The following Monday, Bassett met the players at the RAC Club in London before the squad flew to China for an end-of-season tournament. Watford had been invited back to China since their first visit in 1983 and now they were taking up the offer. But the club was in turmoil. Bassett had a holiday in Spain booked, so he wasn't going to China. Taylor's coaching staff were in the process of following him to Villa and although Bassett was bringing his backroom team from Wimbledon with him, none of them were available to take the team to China.

The physio, Billy Hails, had been told that he was surplus to requirements and would be leaving the club but he decided to go on the trip.

As John McClelland says: 'Billy had been sacked but he said

there was no way he was going to allow the players to go to China, train and play games without a physio. Most people would say, "Bugger off – I'm not going to China if you're sacking me – I'm going on my holidays," but Billy cared about people.'

As the senior member of staff, Hails became the team's manager for the tour, although McClelland felt Bassett missed a great opportunity to get to know his new squad – a decision which caught up with him later.

'It did surprise me that he didn't want to come,' says McClelland. 'On a trip like that you get to know the pecking order of the players, work people out, see them in a more relaxed environment but also get to see them train and play a bit. But he'd booked his holiday, so he didn't come.

'Billy was the manager and we all loved Billy. He'd been the physio for so long and he was just a lovely guy. Some of us senior players – me, Mark Falco, Tony Coton, Luther [Blissett] stepped up a bit to help Billy.'

Watford's previous trip had been to play exhibition games; this time they competed for the Great Wall of China Cup and were based in Nanjing and played in a four-team group with China, Hubei – another Chinese team – and April 25th, which was a team representing North Korea and named after the state holiday that marked the formation of Kim Il-sung's army.

A late Worrell Sterling goal was enough to beat the North Koreans in the opening game and when they went on to beat Hubei and China 2-0, they topped the group to set up a semi-final against another Chinese side, Liaoning.

But, just like in 1983, it was the food, the day-trips and the chance to see the chairman in relaxed mood that left the strongest impression on the players.

'Elton brought about six suitcases – one for hats, one for glasses, one for shoes or whatever,' says McClelland. 'But I did get the feeling that he enjoyed being away as one of the lads. He was known by people in China, I'm sure, but he wasn't mobbed. He wasn't the centre of attention, or the one going on stage every night, with the whole show depending on him.

'Elton was great fun to be around. He joined in with the jokes. There was a piano in the foyer of the hotel and after dinner we'd gather round it making up songs. Luther and I went up to Elton's room and came down dressed in his clothes one night. We just sat down at the dinner table as if nothing was out of the ordinary and Elton was laughing as hard as anyone. He gave me the shirt as a gift, but it got stolen from a dry cleaners not long after.

'It was Elton's generosity that struck me. We were on some kind of tourist's menu in the hotel. Anything Western – Coca-Cola, Fanta, things like that – was very expensive but Elton said, "Have what you want. Put it on my room."'

Watford squeezed past Liaoning in the semi-final with a goal from Blissett and then faced China again in the final. A 2-0 win gave Watford the trophy and made Billy Hails the club's only 'manager' to enjoy a 100 per cent record. Five matches, five wins, a cup the size of a house and a gold watch from Elton were Hails's reward.

'Elton presented Billy with a gold watch at the end of the trip and, looking back, I always regret that we, the players, didn't get Billy something, or get Elton something to say thanks,' says McClelland. 'I do remember the trophy and the medal were enormous. I've always said the lesser the competition, the bigger the medal. I've got a First Division championship medal from my time at Leeds and that's tiny. My medal from China is the size of a saucer.'

Bibliography: watfordfcarchive.com and *The Watford Observer.*

7

Gifton Noel-Williams is the youngest player to score a goal for Watford.

He was just 16 when he hit the net for the first time, against Blackpool in 1996, but, in many ways, he was already a man despite still being a boy.

Life forced him to grow up quickly, and so did football, after he suffered a serious injury when still a teenager.

He defied the odds to play on and, although his career might not have hit all the heights he dreamed of, he was happy to experience what he did.

After spending time coaching in the United States, Gifton has returned to England, and we caught up with him for lunch.

LUNCH WITH GIFTON NOEL-WILLIAMS

Gifton Noel-Williams strides across the restaurant, arm outstretched, in mid-apology for being slightly late. We've arranged to meet for lunch at Lussman's in St Albans but he's had a busy morning and arrives with his 12-year-old son, Isiah.

'You don't mind, do you?' he says as he sits down. 'I've got my boy with me today. He's pretty well behaved,' he adds.

Noel-Williams is 35 now but he could pass for much younger and looks fit enough to still be playing. His hair is long, neatly dreadlocked and tied back loosely, and his smile is big and bright with an almost cartoonish twinkle in the corner thanks to a gold tooth.

He is still the youngest man ever to score for Watford, and the second youngest to play for the club in a competitive fixture. He made his debut against Sunderland at Roker Park in September 1996, when just 16 years and 247 days old. Keith Mercer was 122 days younger than that when he made his debut against Tranmere in 1973. But Noel-Williams scored his first goal, at home to Blackpool in November 1996, 41 days before his 17th birthday. It will take a precocious talent to break that record and Noel-Williams is quietly proud of his place in the history books.

In many ways, though, Noel-Williams was the boy who grew up fast. When he made his debut, he was already tall, broad and strong. He was not intimidated by professional first-team football. Incredibly, he was already a father. His daughter

Daje, the first of his seven children, was born a few weeks before he made his debut.

His childhood prepared him for responsibility too. His father died when he was 13 and, although he had older brothers, he had to step up. His parents split up when he was young and for a few years he took his mother's surname and was known as Gifton Williams. When his father, a Bishop called George Gifford Noel, passed away, he wanted to take his father's surname too.

His was an upbringing defined by family, the church and discipline, all of which stood him in good stead when he started training with Watford as a youngster. Although he was not rated by his first youth-team coach, his cousin Michael instilled in him a determination and spirit of perseverance that led to him catching the eye of Watford's Kenny Jackett.

And, as Jackett rose from the role of youth-team coach to the first team, Noel-Williams went through the ranks with him.

There was, perhaps, the ever-present fear that other youngsters would catch up with Noel-Williams, who was always big for his age, but Jackett insisted he worked on his technique. Luther Blissett helped him develop as a forward in a way that he was able to make the most of his physical strength.

Right from the moment he broke into the team, Noel-Williams made an impression. It is easy to resort to clichés when talking about a striker of his size and stature but nevertheless it is true that he was a handful for defenders, he was good in the air and his touch was good 'for a big man'. He was not necessarily prolific but for a teenager still learning the game he scored his fair share. In the final week of the 1997-98 season, he scored against Bournemouth in the 2-1 win that sealed promotion to the First Division and again at Fulham to clinch the Second Division title.

The following season, as he stepped up to the First Division (now the Championship), he was in and out of the team but had scored 10 goals before the end of January.

And then, he was forced to deal with the sudden prospect that his career might be over at the age of 19. Having scored a terrific goal against the league leaders Sunderland, he was on the receiving end of a bad challenge by Paul Butler. The knee injury was severe enough but he also developed an arthritic condition and was told by bone specialists that if he carried on playing professional football he would end up in a wheelchair.

He fought back and made three appearances in the Premiership, against all odds, then established himself in the team again once Watford had been relegated to the First Division. To an extent, though, he was damaged goods – uninsurable and so very unlikely to play at the top again – but too useful to release.

Eventually, his time at Watford had to come to an end and he left in 2003, with almost 200 appearances, including those as a sub, and 41 goals to his name. He played for Stoke and Burnley and then spent a couple of years in the Spanish Second Division with Elche. After retiring, he went to America to work as a coach before returning to England, where he had done some work with Watford's academy.

He lives in St Albans these days, and as we sit down at the restaurant table, he notices his son Isiah looking uncertainly at the menu.

'They don't do a burger, so choose something else,' Noel-Williams says to him before turning to me. 'He's still American – he's lived in America so long but I'm trying to get him to try some different things.' Turning back to Isiah, he says: 'If you don't like it, you can have some of mine.'

Let's go back to the beginning of your football career, Gifton. Where did it all start for you?
When I was an under-14 they were going to release me from

Watford. The manager of the under-14s at the time didn't like
me for some reason. I didn't used to play no minutes. One day
we were playing Ipswich away. There were four or five of us
London boys at London Euston and all the trains to Watford
were delayed. We rang the manager and said we were going to
be late and he said: 'Don't bother coming.'

I phoned my cousin – God rest his soul, he's passed away
now – and said: 'Michael, all the other boys have gone home.
What should I do?'

He told me to go to Vicarage Road, even though I knew
I'd be too late. I said: 'What's the point? They'll have already
left for Ipswich.'

'Just go to Watford,' he said. 'When you get to the ground,
phone me, then you can come home.'

I said: 'Seriously?!'

So, I went to Watford and walked from the train station to
Vicarage Road and as I was standing there outside the ground,
Kenny Jackett drove past. He said: 'What are you doing here?'
I said: 'I was supposed to be playing for the under-14s but
I was late because the trains were delayed, so they've gone
without me.'

Kenny said: 'Where have you come from?'

I told him I'd come from London and he said: 'You knew
you'd be late but you came all the way anyway? Okay then,
son, you come with me and the under-15s. You can help me
with the kit.'

He played me in the under-15s game, I scored and I think
we won 2-1. Afterwards Kenny said: 'You're not bad, you.
What's your name again?'

There was me and a lad called Daniel Brown, who I
thought was good, but the manager of the under-14s didn't
rate either of us. Daniel was a midfielder, I was a striker and
we played for the same Sunday team. Anyway, the Watford

under-14s manager was sick one day when we were playing
QPR. I must've scored four or five goals and played really
well, and Kenny pulled Daniel and me to the side afterwards
and said: 'You're not playing for this team anymore – it's too
easy for you.'

I said: 'This is the most I've played all season.'

Kenny said: 'Well, from now on, you're with me,' and that
was it – I didn't play for the under-14s any more.

I kept moving up with Kenny. When he moved up to the
under-16s, I moved up, then when he was youth team manager, I played for the youth team. After that, he was the manager
of the first team and he gave me my debut at the age of 16.
So if it wasn't for Kenny, I wouldn't have had the career I had.

**What was it that Kenny saw in you that others didn't, do
you think?**

I think he saw a rawness and I think he saw my family. My
family is kind of crazy, really. Nice people but we like to have
fun and laugh and make noise. My mum used to come to the
games with a tambourine and stuff like that. They loved
Kenny. They'd bring food to matches. I'm not saying that's
what made him want to sign me but he realised I was a good
kid, he saw my family, and he knew I wanted to learn. Me
making that trip from London that day said something about
me. He realised I had support behind me and he knew how
much I wanted it.

I think he saw I had something. Now I am a coach, I see
things that no one else sees. I see a player who might have
what it takes but others don't rate him.

**You were big for your age but there must have been more
to you than that?**

As a young player people did say: 'Yeah, he's good but he's just
big.' My cousin made me work on my first touch. He was adamant that I had to have a good first touch and for a few years

I didn't really work on anything else. I used to watch my cousin play and he'd talk about first touch and movement off the ball, and he kind of brainwashed me. Dribbling past people was quite easy because I was big and strong so I could hold defenders off. I was always playing in the team the year above for my school or my district so I was always being pushed on.

The waiter takes our order. Gifton opts for cod cheeks with garlic, chilli and lime for a starter. Isiah is unsure what to choose so Gifton orders fishcakes and the paella with chargrilled vegetables and halloumi, and says he can take his pick. Gifton tells the waiter: 'I used to live in Spain, so I'll see what your paella is like.'

Having been told his drink of choice, a Guinness, was unavailable, Gifton chooses the Chocolate Porter.

Kenny used to say, 'Don't worry about doing weights – it's all about your feet.' So whenever the other lads went to do weight training, me and Darren Ward and a few others would work on our technique. We'd do skipping or something else that worked on our movement. When I moved up to the men's game, I had confidence in myself because I was strong but I had also worked on my technique and my brain. That's what my cousin and Kenny and all the other coaches who touched me had told me was important. Kenny and my cousin are my two main influences because they taught me the game but Graham Taylor taught me how to be a professional. He said I could do whatever I wanted as long as it got me prepared 100 per cent for the game. Whether you sleep one hour, seven hours or six hours, he didn't mind, as long as it was right for that person and you were ready for the game.

After Graham Taylor and Kenny, I struggled to find coaches like that. I played for some good coaches but those were the ones who taught me. It was like I was in class every day. It was like being in school, and I learned something every day. Even the older guys were learning new things. Even

Gibbo [Nigel Gibbs] and Keith Millen were still learning. It was fascinating to be around. I don't think you appreciate it as much at the time but when I went to other clubs, I realised how good Watford actually was.

Gifton takes a sip of the Chocolate Porter. 'That's nice. Kind of tastes like Christmas.'

What happened to your cousin?

He passed away four years ago. He had brain cancer. It actually happened when I was in America. He got cancer, he recovered and was in remission, then he had a stroke and the cancer came back. It was a sad time for me, a really soul-searching time. It might sound silly but looking back at it now I am glad I was in America when it happened. I think if I'd been here I might have fallen apart. Being in America, I was working a lot, I had my own business. I was there many hours every day, training, coaching, training, coaching, so my mind was focused on something. If I'd been here with time to think it would have been even harder. Talking about it now makes me teary. It was a really hard time because Michael was my mentor.

My dad died when I was 13 so Michael was the person in my life who was always there. He gave me advice, he took me places, we talked about football. He got ill around about the time I had just retired. The plans we had of me doing coaching and him coming over to America to work with me were all gone. I got to know myself a bit more, it brought me closer to my kids and gave me a different outlook on life.

Michael must have filled the gap left by your father as well.

He did. My dad was a bishop. He was 100 per cent about church. He was focused on church. My whole family was church, church, church, but my dad saw football as a distraction, not as a career. He didn't mind me playing football but he didn't really like it. He wanted me to be an accountant.

Are you any good with numbers?

Yeah, I'm good with numbers. I was good with maths so
he wanted me to be an accountant and spend time with the
church. But I have to say, my dad dying made me grow up.
I've got older brothers and younger brothers but I still had to
step up. It made me into a man and it prepared me for everything else. After losing my dad, no matter what anyone told
me, it didn't matter. Whatever anyone said to me, it couldn't
faze me because I'd lost my dad, you know I'm trying to say?
Nothing else can be as bad as that so it kind of prepared me
for what came after – the injuries and my rollercoaster career.
It prepared me for something else so I thank God for the
lessons, really, because I've learned from it.

**So you're from a big family but a close family. And then
you had football, which is a different kind of family.**

Most footballers, their friends are footballers, their wives are
friends with other footballers' wives. I've never lived that life
really. Don't get me wrong – I've got friends who are footballers and my wife is friends with their wives, but most of
my friends are people who I grew up with, people I went to
school with. Our family is quite big. Now we're all older and
have families of our own, we're not so tight-knit but when I
was growing up we were very, very close. That gave me a base
of family. We argue, we fight, we laugh, we joke, we help each
other out. I think that's helped me at difficult times.

You were quite young when you started your own family.

Yes, my career and my family all started young! [laughs]

What age were you?

I was 16. I had my oldest daughter, Daje, when I was 16, then
Dejon, who is at Watford, who is 16 now. There's also Gene,
Niah, Isiah, Frankie-Sienna and Riley, so seven kids altogether.
Four girls, three boys, so I'm still outnumbered. But, yeah, a
lot.

Do you think you've got a big family because you were from a big family?

Yeah, it's normal for me. Last week six of my kids were all together and it was normal. They were all playing with each other, all getting on. It's beautiful to watch as a dad, to see them growing up.

So which came first, your debut for Watford or becoming a father?

It's funny how it worked out but I was a father first. I was still a first-year scholar when my daughter was born. [Gifton runs through all his children's birthdays.] I have got a lot of September birthdays in my family!

The day of my daughter's birth, I had a youth team game in the morning. I played in the youth team and Rob Smith was on the sideline with my phone, just checking it for me. After the game, they rushed me off to the train station and I went into London, and my baby was born in the afternoon.

And a couple of weeks later you were playing for the first team at Roker Park.

It was amazing. I made my debut a couple of weeks later [September 24]. Sunderland away in the Coca-Cola Cup. What happened was there were a lot of injuries. Let's not make no bones about it – that's why Kenny took me on the trip. Honestly, that trip was just to give me some experience – not to play. He said: 'I'm going to bring you along so you can see what the first-team is all about.' We had an overnight stay. It was fun because I wasn't playing, so there was no pressure. Overnight, someone got sick. It was Keith Millen who got sick. Anyway, there were a couple of other options to put on the bench so I wasn't thinking about it. Kenny didn't tell me until the last minute because he didn't want me to get nervous. So all day in the hotel I was just relaxing, doing what I was doing, thinking I'm just going to watch the game and enjoy it.

Then he names the team and my name is down as substitute. My jaw is like this… [Gifton motions his jaw dropping.]
All the boys are saying: 'Well done, well done.'

There was no time to get nervous because I had to get
changed and go out to warm up. I'm still thinking: 'Well,
there's no way I am going to play.' But in the second half, I
was warming up and Luther called me back to the bench and
Kenny put me on. I almost scored as well – I went past the
defender and I was about to hit it and Tony Coton came out
and blocked it.

Can you remember your first goal, against Blackpool?
I was in the box. I got it, I touched it and I turned and shot. I
remember my celebration more. I ran with my hands in the air
like this, straight towards the East Stand, where my family was.
I went and celebrated with them.

**The following season, Kenny Jackett became a coach and
Graham Taylor came back in as manager. What did you
think?**
For me, I was happy. I wasn't happy that Kenny was moving
to the side but he was still coaching so that was good, but I
was happy that I was going to be managed by the ex-England
manager. Many people think one thing about Graham Taylor
but for me personally he's one of the most amazing men I've
ever met. Our relationship was really solid before he became
team manager. The year before, when he was general manager, he found out about my situation with expecting a kid and
he pulled me into his office. All the boys were saying: 'Oh,
the gaffer wants to see you…' and I was wondering what was
going to happen.

He said: 'So, Gifton, how's it going?'

I explained about the whole situation and he said: 'How
are you for money? How are you getting by? Because you can't
be getting by.'

I said: 'I'm trying. I'm trying my best to just get by.'

He said: 'What do you need?'

I told him all the things I needed for the baby and he said: 'How much is that going to cost?'

I said it would be about £300, maybe £400, and he said: 'Are you sure that's all you need?'

He pulled out his personal cheque book. It wasn't a club cheque book – this was Graham Taylor's own cheque book – and he wrote me a cheque for a grand. 'There you go,' he said. 'Make sure you get everything you need. If you need anything else, come back to me. When you are here, I need you to concentrate on football. When you are at home, I want you to look after your baby.'

Before I went in, I thought I was going to be sacked. I'd heard of a lad at another club who'd had a kid young and he'd been fired, although there may have been more to it than that, but I thought I was going to get kicked out.

He said: 'Don't tell anyone about this.' I've kept it from all the boys over the years but now I can say it. Every time I've seen him over the years he asks how my family is, how my mum is. My mum used to love Graham Taylor. She'd give him a big cuddle.

Under Graham Taylor the team improved a lot. You played with Jason Lee and Ronny Rosenthal, and the season worked out brilliantly. You scored the winner against Bournemouth, which helped secure promotion, and then you scored at Fulham, which helped clinch the Second Division title. That must be the highlight of your career.

Oh, a hundred per cent. When I think about those times it still gives me goosebumps. I don't want to be one of those people who keeps talking about the old days but that week, when we won on the Tuesday and then on the Saturday, was one of the biggest weeks of my life.

Now Watford fans knew me properly, Graham Taylor is talking about me, I'm a regular first team player. I was wearing number seven. Big Jason had number nine, Ronny had eleven and Micah had eight. So I was seven, but there was a big fight over that every match day, trust me, because I wanted number nine.

What do you remember about the Fulham game?

Jason Lee crossed it for me and I got in at the near post and got a little flick and it went in. Then they equalised and Jason scored in the second half. That week was amazing. After I'd scored against Bournemouth we were promoted so there was no more pressure.

Before the Fulham game, the gaffer said: 'We have achieved what we wanted to achieve this season. We've got promoted. As a group you have succeeded. Now, how do you want to be? Do you want to go up first or second? Do you want to be champions, or do you want to be known as the guys who just got promoted? How do you want the papers to be writing about you? It's up to you.'

That gets you so fired up. I thought: 'I want to be a champ.'

You don't get a medal for runners-up, do you?

That's what I'm saying. He made us want to win. We went out and we got it. I look at the way Graham Taylor built the team – there's maybe more technical players now, but looking at that time he had the perfect balance. He had youth, like me, he had proven players, like Ronny. He had strength and speed and a bit of skill. The people he brought in were people who were going to teach us. Jason Lee was a teacher, Ronny Rosenthal was a teacher. It was a lovely blend.

Where's your medal now?

At my mum's. Everything is at my mum's. She's got all my

medals going back to when I was an under-eight.

What did you think of the blue and grey away shirt?

Not too sure about it really. I think we should have worn the home uniform but, you know, we'll never forget what we were wearing that day.

The following season you were getting more established in the first team, playing in the First Division. You scored against the league leaders, Sunderland, and then sustained an injury that defined your career. Can you remember the challenge? Did you feel angry about it?

It's a tricky one. I believe that everything happens for a reason – well, maybe not everything, but things happen and how you deal with it defines your character, you know what I mean?

At this point Isiah leans across to swap his paella for the fish cakes. 'That's good, at least you tried it,' says Gifton.

At first it was frustration and worry. Frustration because I knew I'd be out for nearly a year and then worry because I was told I could not play football again. I was told I must retire or else I'd be crippled before I was 40.

What was the injury?

I broke my knee cap but that was actually a fairly minor thing. After the injury, I got arthritis through my whole body. The impact created the arthritis. Sometimes you can have a bad trauma and your immune system can crash and you can get arthritis in your joints because of the shock of an impact. When I first was injured, I couldn't do this. [He demonstrates touching both shoulders with his fingertips.] I couldn't straighten my hands, my fingers were crooked. I was like it for six months. I was on steroids, I was seeing specialists, I was seeing everyone I could and I was being told I would never play again. Then Elton John found out about a medicine in America. He contacted Graham Taylor and Elton paid for me to go to Boston for this treatment, which put the arthritis into remission. For almost a year I was trying to come back and while I was running I was causing damage. The years I was playing I was causing a bit more damage but I didn't care because I was playing. I was playing at Championship level, which I never thought I would be able to carry on doing.

With what happened to me, I shouldn't have played at all, so I thank God for that. I was 19 and I was told I must retire or else I would be a cripple, so there were a few angry nights around that time.

The fact you came back and did play in the Premier League is quite remarkable.

I go back to the beginning of this conversation, when I told you about my dad dying. I thought: 'I coped with my dad dying, so I can beat this. I will play again.' Don't tell me I can't do something, because I've been told that all my life.

My career wasn't as good as the dream was. It wasn't as good as it maybe could have been but I feel I had a good career and some good experiences. But part of my anger was that the week before the injury, I got called up for the England under-21s. I'd played for the under-18s before, but if I had been fit to play for the under-21s, I'd have played with Michael Owen and Michael Bridges. That's not a bad front three, is it?

What do you think about Paul Butler, the Sunderland player who fouled you?

The only thing that I have against him is that he told me he was going to break my leg. It leaves a sour taste in my mouth. You know, he told me he was going to break my leg and he did it. On the flip side, it made me the man I am now.

Centre halves sometimes say that, don't they, to intimidate their opponents? I'm not saying it's right but it happens.

Oh yes, that's my point. I played against Paul Butler four or five times after and I've not got a problem. We had a battle

on the field and we shook hands after. I never tried to get him
back. That's football. My point is, he told me he was going to
do it and I let him do it!

**You played three times in the Premier League but by the
time you were fit to play regularly, the team was back in
the First Division. What was that team like to play in? At
times it seemed like there were four or five forwards on
the pitch.**

Yeah, we had me, Heidar Helguson, Tommy Mooney, Tommy
Smith. Then there was Allan Smart, Nordin Wooter.

It looked fun to play in that team.

Yeah, it was a lot of fun.

**Do you know why a season that had started so well
suddenly hit the wall and then promotion slipped away?**

I can tell you why. Graham Taylor said he was going to retire.
It was the worst thing that could happen. He told us before
the end of the season he was going to retire and for two
months we were sleeping. We were still trying but our leader,
our commander, was going. There was an anxiousness around
the place. The following season [Gianluca] Vialli took over
and that was the worst thing the club could have done.

What did you make of Vialli?

Terrible. Terrible.

Why?

Let me explain this better. From a personal point, for me
as a striker, it was great. I learned so much from him, by
watching him. It was amazing. I'd go to training and he'd be
the best player. He would join in for half an hour and I'd be
like, 'Wow.' His movement was amazing. But as a manager, in
charge of the team and the squad, no. He brought in a lot of
players who, in my opinion, were not as good as the players
we had already, or were just on par. All of us lot got chucked
out and the new players came in. He put some of us back in

the team and we improved but at Christmas he said he was giving the new players another chance. He was too stuck in his ways. I don't think he wanted to admit that some of his signings were not successful.

Were you surprised when he left?

No. It was on the cards and the boys were happy. To be fair, I was excited about Ray Lewington being manager. He was a good coach, a very good coach. But I'm not 100 per cent sure about his man-management skills. He was nice to me and I did enjoy my time under Ray but at the end of his first season I knew I was leaving. I wanted to stay but I understood the situation. I knew he wanted to bring in new faces and freshen it up a bit.

As soon as I realised I couldn't get to the level I wanted to get to in my career, I wanted to stay at Watford all my life, so to leave Watford and go to Stoke was a bit like, 'Oh.'

You know like Lloyd Doyley is a piece of the furniture? I wanted to be a part of the furniture. But by moving to different parts of England, I met so many different types of people. I played in Spain, then I played in America.

What was Stoke like?

Tony Pulis was the manager and I liked Tony. He gave me what I needed. He had a way to play and he was a bit like Graham Taylor in that there was our way to play. If you don't want to do it, that's fine, but you're not going to play. With Graham there weren't arguments because it was clear what he wanted. And if you did what he wanted, he was happy and you were happy. As a player that's exactly what you want because you know where you stand. It's almost like being a child. 'If I want to impress my daddy, I need to make up my bed.' So I make up my bed because I want to impress my daddy. With Graham Taylor I wanted to get into the team so I worked hard. Playing bad was never really part of the discussion with

Graham – it was whether you played hard and put in the work. If you played bad for three or four games in a row, of course he'd pull you aside and say: 'Listen, you're struggling, I'm going to leave you out, but if you work hard it'll come right and you'll get back in.' You can't argue with that. If you are honest and a true professional then you can accept that.

When did you get the gold tooth?

I got it when I was 22. I'd always wanted it because of Ian Wright. He was my idol when I was growing up. He had one, so I wanted one. When I was living in London, near my family, going to church, they didn't really want that kind of thing but when I moved to Stoke, it was like I could do what I wanted. I got my ears pierced, although I don't wear earrings anymore, I got my gold tooth, I got a couple of tattoos.

How did the move to Spain come about?

When I was leaving Watford there was a chance to go to Spain but I wasn't ready to live abroad, or learn the language, so I didn't go. I went to Stoke for two years and then Tony Pulis left so I wanted to leave. I went there for Tony Pulis, really. I didn't have the same history at Stoke that I had at Watford and I'd gone there because of the coach, so when he left, I wanted to leave. I had another chance to go to Spain but I said no again. I was scared of learning a new language, I was scared of something I didn't know, so I went to Burnley. I didn't really enjoy my time at Burnley, so I thought, 'You know what? I'm going to go to Spain.'

Did you learn the language?

Yeah, I got pretty good. I can understand fluently but I struggle to speak it now. Isiah was fluent too, but he's lost it now.

It's a good skill to learn.

Yeah, it's relevant if you want to be a player. You might not play in Spain but you might have Spanish players who come here.

Did you enjoy it?

I loved it. Footballers want to be the best at something or feeling like they are going somewhere. My career had been going upwards but then I was told that no club in the Premier League would buy me because I couldn't pass a medical. When I first got fit and was playing well, Newcastle were interested. My agent got them on the phone and he put it on speaker phone and I heard them say: 'No, we can't sign him because he won't pass a medical.'

So I then had to accept that I was a Championship player, so where's the next step? Stay in the Championship or go and experience something else, whether it's moving up north, or going to Spain or going to America. Even though I wasn't the player I wanted to be I still wanted to learn things, new cultures. Even this stuff... I learned about paella in Spain. It's a small thing but it broadened my horizons. I learned from different coaches. I think the way a Spanish coach works in Spain is different to how a Spanish coach would work here in England because they are in their culture and their way of doing things. In Spain you have a different lifestyle. We'd have days when a guy would bring a huge paella dish in and we'd sit down all together after training, the players and the manager, and have lunch and a beer, maybe two beers. No one was getting drunk – it was nice. That wouldn't really happen in England.

Because no one would want to stop at two beers?

That's my point! It would end up being an all-dayer! [laughs] I played with Argentinians, Bolivians, Uruguayans. I've got friends all over the world now. The Manchester City second goalkeeper, Willy Cabellero – I played with him at Elche.

Why did you go to America?

After I finished playing, I started coaching at Christian high schools in America. I was assistant coach in one, head coach

in another. High schools over there are the size of colleges
over here and colleges over there are huge, like universities
here. I founded my own football club there. I made a load
of mistakes, coaching mistakes, but I have come back here
and I feel I am a better coach for it. Now I'm working for my
Uefa badge and I feel I've got a good basis to my coaching. I
learned so much there about child development, psychology,
how to work with kids.

And in all my free time, I am with my kids. If you see me,
I'm going here or there with one of my kids, or I'm going to
pick them up. It's a full-time job but I love it.

**So tell me about your son, Dejon, who is in the Watford
academy. How does the youth set-up now compare to the
one you came through?**

Goodness! It's different. It's much better in the quality of
facilities and the organisation of it now. The way the academy
system has formed, I think at times it hinders coaches from
really being a mentor as well. The kids get coached very well
every day. In my day, we'd do one day at Vicarage Road and
then we'd do another day at Woodside and that was it. Now
they are getting training sessions three or four times a week,
but I don't think they have the same social side. They are in
a little bubble, almost like little professionals. Do they learn
what real life is about? As I was growing up, I played youth
team football, Sunday league football, schools football, so
there was more opportunities to have a social life, to make
friends and have fun with people from different types of
backgrounds.

The environment I grew up in suited me. Watford was
serious football – you play properly, you don't do flicks and
backheels and all that, but you learn how to play the professional game. But I also had my Sunday team or school team,
and that was fun. I could run around, try all the tricks I'd seen

on television and practise it there. I had the freedom to do
that.

Now, they train three or four times a week – four days
of really good training – but where is the fun aspect of the
game? That's the only difference I find.

So what age is Dejon?
He's 16 now. He's in his scholarship year right now. I took
him out a few months ago because I wanted to make sure his
school work and other aspects of his life were right but now
I've put him back.

What sort of player is he?
I think he plays a bit like me but his feet are softer than mine
and he's not as aggressive as me. I think he's a softer player
than me. Not soft as in a soft touch – just a bit more refined
already.

*The waiter approaches to clear the tables and asks Gifton how he
found the paella.*

GNW: Lovely.

Waiter: As good as the Spanish?

GNW: No, not as good as the Spanish but it was decent.

I think I worked on my technique and got my job done.
My son is technically very good but everything has to be
pretty. I wasn't bothered by that. If it goes in off my knee, it
still counts.

I tell him what Graham Taylor said. I tell him about the
goalscoring areas, where goals are scored from, how many
goals you score with one touch. I tell him until I'm boring
myself! If you score 20 goals a season, ten will be goals that
no one remembers: tap-ins, scrambles. You'll have three or
four a season that are really good goals and three or four that
are pretty nice but most goals are not perfect. They come
off your knee, or the ball comes across the box and you get a
touch on it. No one remembers them but they remember you

scored and they remember the result.

So where are you coaching?

I help out with the academy. I am doing my coaching licence. I am in the system and hopefully I can get a full-time job at Watford. I'd love to work there [at Watford].

With my coaching, I feel I am an apprentice again. When I was a player I was learning, learning, learning, and I got to where I got to. I've done the first part of my coaching apprenticeship in America and now I want to learn more here. I'd love to be Watford's youth team manager. You might laugh at this but I'd love to be first team manager at Watford one day.

Why would anyone laugh at that?

I don't know... I look at Kenny Jackett as my inspiration. He was 28, 29 when he got his knee injury and had to retire. He told me the story of having to retire early and start coaching. He loved coaching and he wanted to be the best he could be at it. And he was never, ever bitter. He said that life goes on after football. I look at all the lessons he taught me and I want to be like that. He started off with the babies, moved up to the youth team, went to the first team, now he's one of the best managers.

What do you think of Watford now?

I look at the team now and think about what they can achieve. I think, 'Go on, Watford.' We were the yo-yo club. We went up and down, and there's nothing wrong with that for the size of the club but now I think we might be able to go up and stay up. They've always developed players and sold them on.

Do you go to many games?

I go to as many as I can. I love being around the place. I kind of disappeared for ten years, didn't I? I went to Spain and America and I've been away from it. So I wasn't in the footballers' bubble. But it's great to come back and see the old faces, like Johnno [Richard Johnson] who's around the club on matchdays. He used to give me a lift home after training when I first started.

Of course, you were 16, you were a dad, you were in the first team but you couldn't drive!

That's right, I couldn't get my driving licence yet!

As a number nine yourself, what do you think of Troy Deeney?

I've been around Troy quite a lot. From the outside, maybe you think one thing about him, but when you meet him he's a really top man. He's a leader, he talks to the young lads. As a player, his record speaks for itself. I think it was unsettling when he had the speculation about a move last summer.

It must be hard when there's the possibility of a big move...

It is. Your heart messes with your head. Sometimes you think about your wallet. Sometimes you think about your career and where you want to be. Sometimes you think about your family and what's best for them. Sometimes your heart takes over and you ask yourself, 'Do I want to leave?' Then he had a couple of injuries, then there were all the management changes. I don't think that at the start of the season he was the real Troy Deeney. But from the turn of the year he's become Captain Fantastic. He's been the driving force. You see him around the training ground and you realise how important he is to the team.

What about Odion Ighalo?

Yeah, he's very good. He's exciting. Him and [Fernando] Forestieri are exciting. You look at Troy and he's the man but you look at Ighalo and Forestieri and they are exciting. What are they going to do? Are they going to shoot from 40 yards and it hits the corner flag? Or will it go in the top corner?

My humble opinion is that they need a couple more workman-like players – good quality but still those players that do all the dirty work for the team. At the moment we play a little bit too much like, 'You have it, we'll have it'. In the Premier League you are going to have to win the ball back. Ben Watson has added some of that. You watch him and he's one of those who does so much but without the fans really recognising it. Every team I've played in has had some of that. I can't remember who it was who called the water carrier?

It was French World Cup winner Didier Deschamps.
That's right. They called Deschamps the water carrier. He carries the water for the whole team while the other ones look good. They're the most important player in the team. That's why Isiah is going to be a holding midfield player...
He's good at that. They are the players who might not get recognised but players talk about them. I will talk about Johnno all day long. He and Micah [Hyde] ran that midfield but Johnno was the one who held it together. Micah would go forward and do the fancy stuff and Johnno held the line, won the ball, gave it easy and kept the team ticking. He brought that stability. Footballers notice those players.

You can be a 'boring' player and make a very, very good career. When I say boring, I mean doing the ugly stuff – all the work that people don't want to do. Without that you can get over-run and lose matches so easily.

If I was coming through now, I'd like to be a holding midfielder. I played that position when I was a kid but one Watford under-15 or under-16 game I was told I could sit out a half or I could play up front. We had too many midfielders and no strikers or something, so I went up front rather than sit on the sideline, scored a couple of goals and that was it – I was a striker.

Watford's still clearly close to your heart. What are your strongest memories now you are retired.
Playing for the team, being successful, meeting the people I

met. Watford is still my club. I am a supporter now. In fact, I remember in 1999, Birmingham City away in the play-offs, I was in with the fans celebrating the penalty shoot-out, and I was at Wembley. It was great. Of course I wish I'd played but I was still there, part of it and it was special. But you know, my journey is my journey. I thank God for what I have had. I haven't got time to regret things, because I have to concentrate on these guys [his children]. I don't go on about my career. Yes, I had a good career – I am in the club of people that played professionally, I played in the Premier League and in under-18 internationals. But I'd love it if one of my kids went on and beat what I did. That's what I say to them: 'Enjoy it and go and beat my career.'

* * *

A few weeks later, we meet again and Noel-Williams tells me his son Dejon was leaving Watford's academy and would be going to Sheffield United's youth system for pre-season training. 'I think it's been difficult for him at Watford,' he says. 'Maybe he needs to go somewhere where his name doesn't mean anything to anyone. He plays up front, he wears number nine, he's 16 and maybe he is aware that his old man played in the first team at a young age.'

Noel-Williams smiles. 'At the end of the day, if he wants it enough and he's prepared to work hard, he's got a chance but I say to all my kids, don't expect good things to just happen to you. You have to go out there and make good things happen.'

It's a good life lesson but it's also hard not to look at Noel-Williams and admire his positive outlook considering everything that has been thrown at him.

There is not a hint of bitterness at what might have been.

Until the next wonderkid comes along, Noel-Williams will

remain the youngest-ever player to score for Watford.

Those who saw him play will have their favourite memories. Perhaps those goals against Bournemouth and Fulham in spring 1998 that helped confirm promotion and then the Second Division title, or a late winner at Chesterfield a couple of months before that, which sparked delirious celebrations on the Saltergate terrace.

But there's another moment that sums him up to me better than any of his goals. Watford were leading Bristol City 1-0 at Vicarage Road on Boxing Day 1998. The visitors had attacked relentlessly for the final 20 minutes in search of an equaliser. In injury time, Watford won a corner and Peter Kennedy rolled the ball to Noel-Williams who shielded it from one, two and then three Bristol defenders before knocking it off one of his opponents to win another corner. Kennedy and Noel-Williams repeated this several times until it became like a pantomime performance with the giant holding off the dwarves. As the Bristol City players lost their rag, a couple of them got booked – one for fouling Noel-Williams, the other for dissent – and the cheers from the Watford fans turned to laughter as he continued to shield the ball until the referee put Bristol City out of their misery by blowing the final whistle.

Noel-Williams strode off the pitch with a big grin on his face – job done, point proved.

8

Think of Wembley in 1999 and, quite rightly, Nick Wright's overhead kick will probably be the first thing that comes to mind.

But with the score 1-0 and the clock running down, Allan Smart was given a chance to settle the nerves and send Watford to the Premiership.

It was a moment when time seemed to stand still for every Hornets supporter. With the ball coming across to him, it required a cool head and an even cooler finish.

Meet Allan Smart, Watford's *other* Wembley hero...

THE OTHER WEMBLEY HERO

> Oh Allan Smart.
> Is wonderful.
> Oh Allan Smart is wonderful.
> Even though he comes from Scotland,
> Allan Smart is wonderful.

As chants go, it's verging on a back-handed compliment but compared to what the supporters at Inverness Caledonian Thistle shouted at him after the merger of the two clubs from the Highlands it must've been like music to his ears.

Let's go back to 1993 and the start of Allan Smart's career. At that time, Inverness had two clubs – Caledonian and Inverness Thistle – playing in the Highland League and both aspiring to join the Scottish League. Officials at the Scottish Football League hinted that a joint application would be more successful and, despite the fact that fans of both clubs were bitterly opposed to a merger, the two clubs amalgamated as Caledonian Thistle and joined the league in 1994. The new club was later renamed Inverness Caledonian Thistle.

While the enmity between the two clubs was not quite on the same scale as the rivalry between Rangers and Celtic in Glasgow, the relationship between the two sets of fans was hostile after the merger was confirmed. Inverness was divided. There were Caley pubs and Thistle pubs. You were either blue and white, or red and black. For most supporters, league football was not worth losing their individual identity for.

Smart was 19 years old and had been at Caledonian only a season, having come up through the ranks of junior football in Scotland, but had scored 15 goals and was doing well until the local paper printed a story saying that the manager, Sergei Baltacha, Allan Smart and a couple of others agreed to the merger.

'I was quoted in the paper as being in favour of it and I'd not said anything at all,' Smart says. 'Inverness is a bit like Carlisle in that it's very close-knit, so it spread like wildfire, and because the merger was not popular I got singled out. For ten months I got abuse off my own fans: "He's white, he's blue, he hasn't got a clue, Allan Smart."

'I scored the winner in the semi-final of the North of Scotland Cup against Ross County, which is a spicy game in the Highlands, and they sang it. Then, in the North of Scotland Cup final – the last ever game as Caledonian before the merger – I scored the winner. We won 1-0 and my goal wins them their last-ever cup but they still sang it. "He's white, he's blue, he hasn't got a clue, Allan Smart." I tell you what, though, it toughens you up.

'It was difficult to start with. I'd come off the bench and my first touch was booed. I was coming home and saying to my mum and dad that I'd had enough, couldn't be arsed with it. Sergei tried to protect me but I couldn't get my head round it. I'd score a goal with a tidy finish and get booed. At the end of the season a book came out and there's a picture of me with the caption, "The man the fans love to hate." I was 19! And I'd never even said it! I just wanted to play football, keep out of it and do my best. The games were difficult sometimes because the crowds weren't that big and the supporters were close to the pitch so you could hear every word. Against Ross County, there were maybe three, three-and-a-half thousand there, so a big crowd for that level. The ball dropped right out of the sky and I hit it first time and I thought, "Right, I'll give it to them," and I went over and gave it all that [he makes a defiant gesture that says, "What about that then? Have some of that."] Then I scored in the final, the last goal as a stand-alone club, and it couldn't get better than that. I hadn't even fallen out with anybody, I'd just been misquoted.'

* * *

First impressions count for a lot in football, and over the course of a 16-year career, Smart had to make a lot of them. It's not being unkind to say that Smart fits the bill of a journeyman footballer, having played for 13 professional clubs, from Caledonian Thistle to Portadown in Northern Ireland. On the way he played for Preston, Carlisle, Watford, Northampton, Hibernian, Stoke, Oldham, Dundee United, Crewe, Milton Keynes Dons and Bury. Have boots, will travel, could have been his motto.

But it was his time at Watford that stands out as the high point of his career – remarkable for the goal that settled nerves at the end of the play-off final against Bolton at Wembley and confirmed a place in the Premiership, the winner against Chelsea and, later in the season, against Sheffield Wednesday. If Tommy Mooney was responsible for two of Watford's six victories in the Premiership in 1999-00, thanks to his goals against Liverpool and Bradford, Smart was responsible for two of the others.

In volume three of *Tales from the Vicarage*, Nick Wright tells the story of how he and Smart ended up moving to Watford in the summer of 1998 after impressing Graham Taylor when they played against the Hornets for Carlisle United a few months earlier. The impression at the time was that

Taylor had bought a job lot of forwards from the Cumbria club's relegation fire-sale, that Smart and Wright came as a package, but that wasn't quite the case.

Carlisle had gone down to the bottom division and Smart had spoken to a few clubs – Swindon and Leyton Orient among them – but was close to joining Northampton, who were managed by Ian Atkins. 'He'd offered me a reasonable deal and I thought it would be a good move because they'd just missed out on promotion when they lost to Grimsby in the play-off final at Wembley,' says Smart. 'But the chairman, Michael Knighton, had met Graham Taylor at a wedding, so the story goes – he did love a story, the chairman, so I don't know if it's true – but he said he'd agreed for me to go down and talk to Watford.

'Michael Knighton was a real character,' he adds of the man who tried to buy Manchester United in the 1980s and famously went onto the Old Trafford pitch and juggled a ball in front of the supporters before the deal eventually fell through. 'He was a fascinating man and I could sit and listen to him all day. He used to come in the dressing room and say, "I've seen aliens on the M62, lads, so anything can happen today."

'I liked it in Carlisle. It's a terrific club and we had a great team with Rory Delap, Matt Jansen, Paul Murray and Scott Dobie who all went on to bigger clubs. It was perfect for me because I could go back to Scotland to see my family. I was settled there but because I could get back up to Perth quite easily to see my family. But going to Watford was a perfect move for me at that time because they were in a higher division. The chairman said Watford wanted me to go for a trial, so he said, "Go down south and meet them, will you?"

'We met Graham at the Jarvis hotel, in a suite, down a corridor in an exclusive part of the hotel. I wanted to create a good impression so I got suited and booted. I thought they wanted me to go on trial but the first thing the gaffer said was he wanted to sign me and did I want a three-year contract or a four-year contract? That was his opening gambit and I just sat there bemused. I said I'd take the four-year deal and he sat and spoke to my missus for the best part of an hour. She's my ex-wife now… It was a great deal for her, really. She's done all right out of it…'

A year before signing for Watford, Smart had played 24 minutes of the Auto Windscreens Shield final for Carlisle against Colchester before having to go off. He had picked up an injury weeks before the game and had not realised he'd been playing with a cracked ankle. 'I'd taken anti-inflams [anti-inflammatories] to get through games and how I blagged the fitness test for the final, I'll never know. I loaded myself up… the abuse of anti-inflams was ridiculous but it was a cup final. I thought it was my only chance to play at Wembley and I'd do the exact same thing again, although looking back it's very selfish. But I wanted to play. I felt a bit guilty because the lads knew I was touch and go on it but the gaffer [Mervyn Day] asked me how I was and I said that if I got rattled on it, I'd be knackered, but if not, I was good to go. He asked me what percentage I put myself at and I said 80, 85, 90 per cent at a push but then, after 20 minutes, I got smashed on the ankle and that was it. I remember sitting on the bench in tears and the Sky camera was in my face asking how I felt. How do I feel? Are you having a laugh?'

When Smart met Graham Taylor, a dark thought lurked in the back of his mind that the ankle injury might show up in the medical and cost him the move to Watford.

'The thing was, it was back in the day when finances were tight and scans and things like that were expensive. With my catalogue of injuries I'd have cost the club a bloomin' fortune in medical bills. I had a bit of ultra-sound, a bit of ice, a bit of rest, some anti-inflammatories and I played on.

'The gaffer [Taylor] was offering me the biggest deal I'd ever seen, for four years. He's dangled the lottery ticket in front of me because I was on two-bob and a Kit-Kat at Carlisle. I thought my ankle was going to let me down.

'I did my medical, went back to the Jarvis and I couldn't eat, I couldn't sleep. I got back to my bedroom and there was a note on the floor by the door. "Don't worry about the medical, the next four years are going to be great. I'm signing you, Graham Taylor." He called me the next morning and said, "I bet you still didn't sleep, did you?" After I put the phone down, I felt like Pele. Honest to God, he made me feel like the best football player in the world.'

The results of the medical were delayed and Smart was having kittens, despite Taylor's reassurances. 'The gaffer was working for the media at the World Cup in France and he rang and left a message, "Hello, it's Graham Taylor here. I hope you're keeping fit, hope you're enjoying the summer and preparing for your wedding..." He went on and on and on but it was lovely. I saved the message and played it to my dad: "That's an England manager wanting to sign your son." I kept that message for weeks, months, and I played it to everyone. I was buzzing but I still hadn't signed and I thought it would be just my luck something will go wrong.

'Eventually, the medical is all done, good to go. I'm getting married on July 4, pre-season training is starting on July 6 but the gaffer had told me to go for a fortnight's holiday but I said, no – I said I'd go back to the Jarvis and start pre-season on the sixth. On my wedding day, my best man is doing the telegrams and there was a message from all the staff at Watford FC. There were some John Lewis vouchers, a hundred quid's worth or something.

'So, when people ask why you'd run through a brick wall for

Graham Taylor, that's why. I'd have run into a brick wall until he told me to stop. I defy anyone to walk away from him when he wants to sign you and I think that's the biggest compliment I can pay.'

* * *

When Smart first spoke to Taylor about his role in the team, the manager asked him how he saw his role in the team. 'I'd not really expected to be asked what I thought,' says Smart. 'So I just said, "Well, I can link the play. I can play off the shoulder of a big number nine and I'll get my fair share of goals but I won't be your top goalscorer." The people who played with me scored goals and I chipped in but I linked the play up because I could control the ball well. Managers would ask me to come short and show for the ball because I had a good first touch. I said I wasn't the quickest and I wasn't going to get in behind that often, and I wasn't that great in the air and he [Taylor] just said: "I'm not interested in what you're not good at. I'm going to focus on what you are good at and everything else will come up."

'I believed from an early age that you only have to be good at two or three things to be a good football player. You don't have to be Messi. If you're a good tackler, you could be a pro. If you're good at heading the ball, you could be a pro. If you're good controlling the ball, or reading the game, you could be a pro. You don't have to have all five things and I kind of got that into my head early on because my old man used to say that if you could control the ball and not give it away, you will be a commodity for someone, and he was right.

'Growing up, it was almost an obsession not to give the ball away. I scored goals anyway, so I took pride in linking the team up, holding the ball, giving it to a team-mate. My old man gave me a tennis ball in the garden and said, "Keep the tennis ball up for 100 and then volley it and come in and see me," and I'd be out there for an hour and a half trying to keep this tennis ball up. That stuck with me throughout my career: just make sure the ball is under your control when it comes to you, and keep it under control and away from the opponent.'

When Smart was growing up, his father was involved with Scottish non-league football in Perth as a manager with Jeanfield Swifts, so he soaked up a lot about the game at a young age. 'I would go on the team bus, I'd sit in on the team talks, I'd clean the boots on a Sunday so that's been embedded, really,' he says. One thing he didn't get from his dad was a fiery temper. 'I think that's more from my uncles on my mum's side,' he says. 'I'm a bit of a rocket, temper-wise. I'm strong-willed and I'll give an opinion. I'll say what I think.'

One example of that came after his debut for Watford, away at Portsmouth on the opening day of the 1998-99 season, on their return to the division that's now known as the Championship. Watford won 2-1 but Smart was replaced midway through the second half, while Watford trailed 1-0. 'The gaffer comes round afterwards and shakes everybody's hand. In the first half-hour, Portsmouth were brilliant. John Aloisi was magnificent. He cut in from the left and just scored a great goal. It was roasting hot, the pace of the game was something I wasn't used to and they were battering us. Anyway, I get hooked and when he shook our hands I said something like, "I was shit." He didn't say anything but on the Monday at training in Stanmore, the gaffer was watching with Tom Walley. He called me over and said: "Did I hear you right on Saturday?" I apologised and said that I knew I'd been absolute crap. He said he didn't think I'd been that bad and then he told me I was going to be playing – that I was his number nine, so I was just going to have to get on with it.'

One of Smart's early partners was the unconventional Michel Ngonge – one of the few players Taylor ever signed without watching him play live, choosing instead to go on a series of video tapes. As Taylor says: 'You can edit someone to look like a world-beater on video.'

Smart had high expectations of himself but Ngonge's more carefree attitude to the game taught him something.' He was an infectious character and a really smiley bloke and in a funny way we complemented each other,' says Smart. 'If the ball went six inches away from where it was supposed to go, it would piss me off. Because I could control the ball, because that was my game, when my touch was off it annoyed me. When I was having a stinker and the ball was coming into feet and it wasn't sticking, my body language would deflate and I'd be struggling to stay on the pitch. But Michel was completely the opposite. He could be in a phone box with four other people and come out with the ball and not know how he did it. The ball would hit his knee, his chest, his shin but he'd get past people. His enthusiasm and completely opposite outlook to mine meant he could ricochet past everyone. He could fire one in the top corner but if it went a mile over the top he didn't beat himself up about it.'

It took Smart a few weeks to settle into the team and he counts the 4-1 win at Bristol City as the turning point. He held the ball up well, linked the team together and Richard Johnson hit two belters. A few days later he scored his first goal, to put Watford 1-0 up at the Stadium of Light. 'Michel laid it on a plate – unbelievable, it was like a miracle – just a nice little roll, I stepped onto it and happy days. I scored my first home goal against Queens Park Rangers and that settled me down, then I scored a couple at Swindon – a nice little volley and then one where Gibbo [Nigel Gibbs] played a little ball in to me, I chested it and flighted the ball over the keeper with the laces – a tidy finish. After that I felt I was part of the team.'

By now he felt he had been accepted by the supporters, which was important to him after his experience with the merger in Inverness. 'It's massive to get on with the fans but, then again, I am the type of player some people will like and some won't, so I am used to listening to the only person at the club that really counts – the gaffer,' he says. 'I think people have their favourites. You can sit in the stands and there's a player you don't particularly rate and it doesn't matter what he does, you're not having it, yet there's a player that you like and when he's not playing well, you make an excuse for him.

'Fans usually have a look at a new player and they're checking him out, aren't they? What does he do? I say to lads now that if they play what I call "clap" football, they'll do all right. By that I mean do the things that'll get you a clap. You realise that you can dictate how people feel about you. You can actually control the crowd. If you put in some effort and close down the keeper, you'll get a clap. If you run a hundred yards to close someone down or chase a ball and keep it in, you'll get a clap. The same with your choices in a game. If you get the ball wide and you get down the side and cross it in with your second or third touch, you'll get a clap. If you check back, check back, check back and then lose it, the crowd will groan. Supporters know what the aim of the game is. If you win the ball back, cross the ball, get it into a decent area, or shoot, even if it goes over the bar, you'll get a clap. The more you do that, the more times you're doing the right thing. Tommy [Mooney] was always one for running to get the ball when we had a throw-in, for looking like he wanted to get on with it. We took the mickey out of him for it but that's Tommy managing the crowd, getting them on his side.

'I remember hearing someone talk about another player saying that his 'bad' game wasn't good enough to get him a transfer. By that I mean that if your worst game is still six or seven out of ten instead of three or four, you're of more value to the team. And even when things aren't going for you, you can turn a five-out-of-ten performance into a six or seven by working harder. That's how you define a professional footballer, I think. There's a lot of talented lads who don't make it, or who slip out of the pro game after two or three years.'

* * *

Watford fans have every reason to be grateful for Allan Smart's fiery streak. The game against Tranmere Rovers in April 1999 has attained a legendary status for its importance in kick-starting the run to the play-off final. Before that, Watford were more or less out of contention; after it, the team was galvanised, together and willing to scrap for the cause. In Smart's case, literally.

The Hornets were drawing 1-1 when Richard Johnson was sent off with ten minutes to go, which sparked a melee and an argument on the bench. Then, with three minutes left, Watford were awarded a penalty and the game erupted again. Smart picks up the story.

'The gaffer started the game by saying we had to win 12 games to get promoted,' says Smart. 'He said that's where it's at, so deal with it. It was 1-1, nearly the end of the game, and we got a corner and it was my job to go and stand right on top of the keeper to stop him coming out to get the ball. Anyway, I thought, "I'm going to stand on his toes here," so I stepped on his toes and dug my heels in. He pushed me and the ref gave a penalty kick. It was shitty – I make no bones about it. I've planted my studs on his toes but sometimes you've got to do what you've got to do.'

Finally, after more argy-bargy and a long delay, Peter Kennedy's weak penalty was saved by the Tranmere keeper,

John Achterberg, only for Ngonge to follow up and score what turned out to be the winner. While some of the players celebrated, Smart was engaged in a proper punch-up with Tranmere's David Kelly. 'He got a swing in from behind and there was just a bit of handbags,' is Smart's assessment. 'Someone else had a swing at me and then it was boom – no bones about it – straight red card.

'I came into the dressing room thinking the gaffer was going to go ballistic but obviously Johnno was already in there, and he was still raging. But Johnno was the teacher's pet – the gaffer loved him – so I thought, well, he can't have a go at me and not him.

'When the gaffer came in, he pointed to me and Johnno and said, "You and you, magnificent, we needed something to kickstart our performance. Now, your punishment is going to be trying to get back into the team after your suspension.'

Smart lost his regular place in the team as a result of his suspension and didn't start another game that season, although he came off the bench in both legs of the play-off semi-final against Birmingham City.

The build-up to the away leg at St Andrew's was far from ideal. 'We had our pre-match meal at The Belfry and then got stuck in traffic going to the ground. The gaffer hated getting to the ground early but we were running really late and had to get a police escort up the hard shoulder. We only got there 40 minutes before kick-off and Chambo [Alec Chamberlain] was raging. He was one who liked to be there in good time, and for a goalkeeper preparation is a massive thing. Our dressing rooms were in a Portacabin because they were doing building work at the ground. I got changed and it felt like everything was a real rush job.

'I was sub and I hadn't even got to my seat when Birmingham scored. I felt a shudder when they scored. The place was rocking. I've been at Ibrox, Celtic Park and Hampden Park. I've been at the old Celtic Park on the terrace behind the goal so I've witnessed some big atmospheres but I felt a shudder in the ground that night and, honestly, I feared the worst.

'But we dug in. Chambo was outstanding and made several big saves but the team as a whole defended well. It was like we were a man down and I can remember looking at the body language of the lads and could tell they were just wanting something to happen that would stem the tide. Birmingham were superb without getting the scoreline to reflect it. They threw everything at us and I always felt we could nick something but I just felt it was always going to go to penalties.

'And I just knew I was going to get on the pitch to take a penalty. I don't think I've hit as many penalties as I've hit in the weeks that led up to that game. I hit hundreds of them. I hit the same penalty over and over again but I didn't feel like I was mastering it. Some were three-feet inside the post, some went straight in the side of the goal, some were a bit high, but I knew I didn't want to be the person who hadn't practised. I wanted to wake up that morning knowing I had done what I had to do.

'I didn't want it to fall on my shoulders if we didn't go through. I think in that situation you need a banker penalty. I wasn't a regular penalty taker and I'm not talented enough to walk up with 30-odd thousand people in the stadium and decide what to do in the spur of the moment. So my logic was that I wanted to try to nail my penalty down to the floor and I chose to go to the keeper's bottom right – bottom left as I'm looking at the goal.

With the shoot-out into sudden death and the score tied at 5-5, it was Smart's turn to step up. Everyone on Watford's bench knew where he was going to put his penalty. Now it was all down to whether the Birmingham goalkeeper dived the right way or not.

'That rattled the gaffer because he knew where I was going to put my penalty. It had got to the point in training where we'd be doing a penalty shoot-out and Chris Day [the reserve goalkeeper] was just walking across and catching my shot because he knew where it was going.'

There was sound reasoning behind Smart's thinking. 'For me, practice can't be random,' he says. 'I wanted to practise my penalty so I could rely on it in those circumstances. You're not talking about a penalty in a game where we're 3-0 up and it doesn't matter – this is a penalty in sudden death. If I missed it, we could be knocked out. So I didn't want to be walking up to the ball in two minds. I didn't want to have to decide as I was putting the ball on the spot what I was going to do. If you watch me as I put the ball down against Birmingham, I'm just looking at the ball. I don't take my eyes off the ball. I'm reading, "Mitre. Mitre. Mitre," on the ball. I remember the lad who taught me to play golf told me the way to keep my head down was to read the name on the ball. "Titleist. Titleist. Titleist." This was the same thing.

'I was confident about my penalty. I couldn't control what the goalkeeper was going to do but I was confident the ball was going inside the post, as close to the post as possible without being risky. If I was going to miss that penalty it was because the goalkeeper had guessed the right way and saved it. That's the lottery everybody takes but I was not going to miss my target. I wasn't a regular penalty taker for the team so there was no way the goalkeeper was going to know which way I'd go unless someone in our team told him, so that was it. I was quite happy living or dying by that decision.'

Smart rolled the ball into the corner, the Birmingham goalkeeper dived the other way. He turns, points to his team-mates and then cups his ear to milk the cheers. Meanwhile, Sky's director cuts to Graham Taylor in the dugout. There's barely a flicker on his face. A few minutes later, Alon Hazan scored to make it 7-6 and Chris Holland missed for Birmingham, which sent Watford to the play-off final at Wembley.

* * *

After that it was a case of waiting to see who Watford's opponents in the final would be. When Bolton defeated Ipswich, Smart began to believe he was destined to reach the Premier League.

'I was really upbeat about playing Bolton because, out of the two of them, I thought they suited us much more,' he says. 'We'd played Bolton at Vicarage Road a few weeks before and we absolutely battered them. I don't know what the other lads thought, but I fancied us against Bolton. Ipswich were a different animal and I wasn't so sure about them. I thought we might find it harder against them, I don't know why, but that was just the feeling I had.'

Then it was a case of waiting for confirmation that he'd be involved in the game. In those days there were only three substitutes. One would be a goalkeeper, just in case. In all the matches leading up to the final, Alon Hazan and Smart had been the two outfield players on the bench.

'I knew if I was named on the bench, I'd get on the pitch because of the way we played. A couple of the lads would run and run until they had no legs left, so I knew we were definitely a 13-man team. I was pretty confident I would be on the bench but on the morning of the match he'd not named the subs so I still wasn't sure. I knew Hazan would be one because he could hold the ball. I just hoped he wanted an attacking player rather than a defender.

'Me and Wrighty [Nick Wright] were sitting outside the hotel after breakfast and all the wives, girlfriends and parents were all getting ready to go off to Wembley because they were leaving before us. Anyway, we saw this guy running down the road towards us, jogging, in all this bright yellow gear and we thought, "Look at the state of him…" Anyway, it wasn't until he got closer that we realised it was the gaffer! He'd gone out for a run. He stopped and had a little chat with us, just small-talk, and I was half-expecting him to tell me to stop worrying and that I was on the bench, but he didn't say anything.

'A little bit later on, I said to Wrighty, "Do you know what? I fancy you to score today." He hadn't scored for a while [not since February 20] and he hadn't really looked like scoring either, to be fair, but I just said it because while I was worrying about whether I'd get a game, I just wanted to say something positive to a team-mate. I don't think it has any bearing on any-thing but it didn't hurt. I just wanted to perk him up a bit, let him know I believed in him.

'We'd had our pre-match meal and still the gaffer has not announced the subs and I am starting to go nuts so I said to Pagey [Robert Page, the captain], "Hey, go and ask him if I'm on the bench because I am going mad here." Pagey came back and said, "Yeah, same subs."

'It was such a relief because until you know, there's still a doubt and some managers can be idiots about things like that. Not Graham Taylor, but other managers have thrown in a real random one at one o'clock on match day.'

* * *

'If you're going to score at Wembley, you might as well do it after a guy has scored a worldy of an overhead kick, eh?'

Smart is only joking when he rolls his eyes and suggests he rues the fact that Nick Wright's acrobatic goal gets most of the attention from that play-off final. Besides, his goal was just as important because it wrapped up the game just when Watford were at their most vulnerable.

Smart was warming up when the ball flew to Wright and he launched himself into the bicycle kick. 'I was right in line with it and when he turned to celebrate he was running right towards me and I was giving it loads. It was a hell of a strike.

'The second half was really nervy. If Bolton had equalised, how would we have responded? I think it was absolutely vital that we held on. I knew as the game went on that I'd get on because our forwards had been doing so much work.'

With 15 minutes to go, Graham Taylor motioned to Smart to get ready. He was being sent on to replace Michel Ngonge. As Smart is preparing to run on, Taylor is talking to him. What was the manager saying?

'I have no idea,' says Smart. 'I can't remember. I was in my own world. He could have been speaking Chinese or Dutch. I don't know what he was saying but to be honest I didn't need to be told to do anything. I knew exactly what needed to be done – go on the pitch and help the boys. Win the ball, hold the ball up, don't give it away, buy us some time and keep our shape. You can see on the video I'm nodding but I can't remember a word. I'm pretty sure he wasn't telling me to get on there and score a goal in the last minute!

'At that point, with 15 minutes to go in a Wembley final, 1-0 up, the gaffer is putting you on the park because he trusts you. It boils down to trust. He knew I wasn't going to go on there and do anything silly.

'I got on the pitch and I tell you, within minutes I was blowing out of my pipe. A big game can do that to you. You're like a wind-up toy waiting to go on and then you sprint onto the pitch, you sprint two or three times to close someone down and suddenly it catches up with you. Sometimes the hardest shift in football is to come off the bench and get into the game. It took me four or five minutes to get my second wind.'

Watford were hanging on and in the dying minutes the ball broke loose just outside the centre circle in their half of the pitch. It wasn't quite a 50-50 ball because it was closer to Bolton's Scott Sellars than it was to Smart but both players went in wholeheartedly. You could almost hear the crunch from the other side of the stadium.

'I went in hard, he went in hard,' Smart says. 'I don't think I even looked to play the ball, to be honest, and I don't think either of us got a touch on it. I've had my leg broken a couple of times and I went in hard to look after myself. I didn't try to do him but I did go in hard. The referee could have given a free-kick either way but because it was 50-50 he let it run. The ball fell to me and Micah, and I let him have it and he plays a lovely ball to Peter Kennedy. As soon as Micah plays the ball, I am running into the channel.

'A few minutes earlier, the ball had broken to Peter on the left and he had a shot that hit the side-netting when I was in the area, six yards out, waiting for the tap in. I was giving him grief after that, yelling, "You greedy so-and-so," just having a right moan. Whether he heard a word of it or not, I don't know.

'Anyway, this time, Peter took one touch and then rolled it across to me. As the ball came to me, one word was in my mind: "Contact. Contact. Contact." I was just concentrating on getting a good contact on it. If I got a good strike on it, I knew the goalkeeper had a problem. I didn't pick my spot, I just hit it with the outside of my boot and I got a lovely contact on it and it flew in.'

That sparked the celebrations of a lifetime for Smart, whose pregnant wife was in the stands, and his team-mates.

'Afterwards, I had to go and do the TV and the press conferences and although I wouldn't change it for the world, I wish I'd put the press on the back burner and celebrated with the

lads first. The big players get that every season, which I'm en-
vious of. I loved games like that, occasions like that, but they
come round so rarely. After we'd done all the press, it was just
me and Wrighty in the bath. Everyone else had got changed
and was with their families. Kenny [Jackett] stood next to the
bath and said: "Two hundred and fifty grand from Carlisle, eh?
Not too bad." I liked to wind Wrighty up and say I was worth
200 and he was the 50.

'To have played at Wembley twice, to have won twice and to
have scored. That's nice to have and it's nice to be taken back
to that time so I can remember it. The gaffer used to say I was
a dour Scot, and he's probably half right, but I do enjoy these
memories.'

* * *

It has been well documented in this book and previous editions
in this series that the team that won promotion to the Premier
League was hit by a string of serious injuries. Smart was one of
those who feels he didn't really get a fair crack at the top flight.
'Peter Kennedy, Nicky Wright, Gifton, Tommy Mooney all got
injured. Johnno was injured a lot. I couldn't believe the gaffer
let Baze [Darren Bazeley] go. He got a good offer from Wolves
and I think sometimes when you're the young boy who comes
through from the youth team, you're the one who gets mugged
off when others come in on more money. I don't know the full
story but I do know we missed Baze because he was quality.

'That summer I got an injury. It wasn't a serious injury but I
did my tendon at the top of my ankle and it was giving me a lot
of gyp. I was going into the biggest season of my life and I had
this problem, and I was like a raging bull. I put a lot of pressure
on myself because I hated being injured.

'I'd been brought up in an environment where if you were

injured you just played through. I have to take things for my stomach now because of anti-inflammatory abuse. I was taking 15, 16 tablets before a game some days. I'd take five or six to go and train, but that was the era, wasn't it? I played with cracked ankles. I played with broken toes. They used to have this rub at Carlisle that had chilli in it. It was an irritant so instead of feeling like you had a bruise or a strain, it felt like you'd burnt yourself and you could play. I used that on my big toe – the big toe I can't bend now – for weeks.

'So when my ankle injury cropped up, I was pushing myself to get fit. I didn't really get on well with the physio. I don't think he trusted me. I remember the gym was the size of a closet and when you were in there day after day it really wasn't an inspiring place to be. I wanted to go to Lilleshall to get fit because I knew you worked from nine till three on your rehabilitation every day but I didn't go there.

'One day at Watford, I asked if I could go out on my bike instead of ride on the static bike in the gym. I just wanted to get out for a change of scenery and do my work, so I went out on my bike for an hour and a half and when I got back, because my T-shirt wasn't wet with sweat, the physio didn't believe I'd done anything.

'I had no respect for him after that. I'd been all round town, up and down the canal, up hills and everything and he was treating me like an apprentice trying to cut corners on a nine-lap run? I wasn't having that.

'I wanted to play in the best league in the world. I wanted to be fit. If doing 500 reps on the weights was going to help me, I'd have done 500 reps. I didn't need some numpty standing over my shoulder counting to 20. When I was a part-time player at Inverness I drove 300 miles a week to get to training, so do me a favour. I couldn't wait to get out of that treatment room and start playing.'

* * *

Smart's first Premier League game was a few weeks into the season, at Upton Park in the 1-0 defeat to West Ham. 'I had a couple of little half-chances,' he says. 'I remember catching one well in the first half and David James got down to it with his left hand. I thought that would have been a goal at a lower level but that was the difference.'

Seven days later, though, Smart felt he had arrived. The day before the Chelsea game at Vicarage Road, Graham Taylor told Smart he'd be leading the line with Peter Kennedy and Nordin Wooter supporting from wide positions. 'That was as good a game as I'd played from start to finish. My touches were good, my feet felt sharp and I just felt that all the work I'd done to get fit was paying off.' Smart scored the only goal of the game, with another shot with the outside of his right foot.

During the week that followed, there was speculation he was in line for a call-up to the Scotland squad for their Euro 2000 qualifiers against Bosnia and Herzegovina, and Lithuania. The following Saturday, his fledgling Premier League career was on hold after he was on the receiving end of a bad challenge at Highbury.

'I was starting to think I was going to get the call from Scotland,' he says. 'I'd got some good exposure from the goal at Wembley and now from the Chelsea goal, and a few old Scottish players were saying, "Well, the boy is Scottish and he's scored a couple of decent goals in big games..." People were starting to take a bit of notice of me. But a few days later I was in the infirmary and the guy shouldn't have been on the park anyway.'

In the first half against Arsenal, Smart was through on goal with the Gunners goalkeeper, Alex Manninger, rushing out towards him. The foul that followed was not too different to the famous one the German goalkeeper Harald Schumacher committed on the Frenchman Patrick Battiston in the 1982 World Cup semi-final. There's a photograph of Manninger's challenge on Smart in the book *Four Seasons*. Both players are in the air, Manninger's knee is up high. Smart's body is half-turned away from the impact and his eyes are closed.

'I lifted the ball over him,' says Smart. 'I don't even know where the ball went – it must've ended up on the top of the net. But he wiped me out and I think I was knocked out for a few seconds. But I was thinking, "Well, at least that's a penalty and the goalkeeper sent off." That should have been a red card but we were at the Clock End at Highbury, so that's not happening. We didn't get a penalty either.

'So, early in the second half Martin Keown went to head the ball back to Manninger and I read it and I thought the goalkeeper was never going to get there. He dived full length to try to get the ball but I flicked it past him and he's gone straight into my leg like Superman. My leg went that way, where it doesn't want to go, and I knew I'd done my knee. The thing was that he shouldn't have been on the pitch after the first foul.

'And that was it. My knee was never the same again after that. That's seven days in your life, right there. People are talking about me getting a call-up for Scotland and then I'm out for nearly five months.'

Smart's goalscoring touch returned when he got back into the team in the spring. He scored four in six games, which counts as prolific in a Premier League team that managed fewer than a goal a game that season.

After his winner against Sheffield Wednesday, Smart struck a pose mimicking the kilt-wearing shot putter on the Porage Oats cereal box. 'There was an advert on at the time where it's snowing and the guy is walking down the street in his kilt and a vest and the wind blows his kilt up while a couple of women are there and the line goes, "There's oats and there's oats, but there's only one Scott's Porage Oats." I used to joke to the missus about that so I thought, "I'm having that. I'll do that the next time I score."

'I wasn't one for doing a big celebration but that's the Premier League, isn't it? I think it brought out a different side of my personality. So when I scored, my missus was in the stand, so I did that celebration. The next thing, a pallet of Porage Oats turns up at the house and the guy who's in the advert was there for a photo opportunity and he said, "I tell you what, mate, you've saved me from eviction!"'

* * *

The injuries to key players didn't help, but Watford were battling to survive on all fronts in the Premier League and Graham Taylor was hoping to strike it lucky with something. He signed Charlie Miller, a gifted but wayward Scottish midfielder who could give Paul Gascoigne a run for his money on all fronts. Here's a bit of Charlie Miller trivia: when David Beckham scored from the halfway line for Manchester United against Wimbledon at Selhurst Park in 1996 he was wearing Miller's boots, which were embroidered with the word 'Charlie'. Miller had a boot deal with Adidas. Beckham needed some boots and, because they were the same size, they sent Miller's boots to the Manchester United player by mistake.

'That shows you how talented Charlie was,' says Smart, who played with Beckham when he was on loan at Preston North End. 'Charlie had a boot deal with Adidas, he had his name on his boots, and he had been player of the year at Glasgow Rangers. He was a serious talent, a great, great football player, but we never saw the best of him at Watford. I was with him at Watford and Dundee United and we never actually started a game together because I was injured when he was in the team at Watford and I never played at Dundee United, but he was great to play with in training. He'd find a pass that no one else could find. He'd thread it through the eye of a needle for you.

'He was a completely different player to Beckham but they were both incredible at putting the ball wherever it needed to be. Beckham turned up at Preston on loan when I was there. He was just a kid and he had the lot. He came in on the Friday and the manager said, "Listen up, this lad is going to be taking all the set-pieces, all the corners and free-kicks, okay?" Ian Bryson, who was the captain, threw his toys out of the pram. "This kid's on loan from Manchester United and he's going to take all the set-pieces on his debut? Are you sure? He's not taking free-kicks off me." So at the end of training, Beckham just took a bag of balls and he's pinging them wherever he wants to. If you asked him to land the ball on that blade of grass, he'd land the ball on that blade of grass.'

As gifted as Charlie Miller was, he did not fit in to the Taylor regime too well. He came south from Glasgow with a reputation for enjoying a night out.

'Charlie was asked to do a diet sheet when he first arrived,' says Smart. 'He had to put down everything he was eating and drinking and Charlie, bless him, was 100 per cent honest and I think that went against him.

'We all went to Portugal for a few days in January and it went a bit pear-shaped. The idea was to have a few days' break just for a change of scenery, some good training in decent weather. We had a day off and we were given the chance to do whatever we wanted. Eight or ten of us went golfing, another eight or ten went straight to the bar. The gaffer was quite happy with that as long as everyone kept it sensible but when he saw the state of a certain fellow countryman [Miller], that was it. I can still see him walking straight into a glass door and I was thinking, "Oh no, not in front of the gaffer."

'The gaffer said there was no more drinking for the rest of the trip. The thing is, we were all footballers and there's some egos and that's what it's all about at certain times. If someone says, "You can have a drink," we will think, "Okay then, let's have a proper drink." There's no in between. No, "Let's go for a couple." It's about who can be last to bed but first up for training. I'm not saying all the time at all but when you get a group of young men at the peak of their game they think they're invincible. But after that we were treated like school kids and I was never the best when it got like that. I was an adult. If I wanted to go out, I'd go out. I knew what the limits were. I knew when it was important to be totally serious and when you could let off a bit of steam.'

* * *

After relegation to the First Division at the end of the 1999-2000 season, Smart found it hard to get back into a team that had made a blistering start to the season and were neck-and-neck at the top with Fulham. 'I was fit and I was playing really well in the stiffs [reserve team]. I scored a lot of goals and the gaffer had said he was coming to watch me. "You're not far away," he said. I would always go and knock on his door – not to say, "I'm better than the guys who are in the team," but to say I was ready to play.

'It just went on a few weeks too long and I couldn't get my head around it. I had always played whenever I'd been fit and, looking back, I just couldn't handle not being in the team.

'Ronny Rosenthal was my agent at the time and he was into me, saying I had to speak to the gaffer to force the issue a bit. I had people saying that this club wanted me or that club wanted me. I was speaking to Moyesy [David Moyes] about going back to Preston. He was the gaffer there but he'd been a player when

I was there before. He was saying he was keen but he could only go so far on me – 600 grand or whatever it was. He was asking what I wanted to be paid.

'Looking back, I was stupid listening to all that. Really, I should just have got on with my job and if someone came in for me and I moved, I moved. That was my mentality all along but I was getting more and more wound up and annoyed that I wasn't playing. It was never about money or anything – I just wanted to play.

'I scored a load of goals for the stiffs against Chelsea and I thought, "Right, well I'm surely playing on Saturday." We were playing Burnley and I wasn't in the team. It got postponed right before kick-off because of a waterlogged pitch but that was it for me. I'd give my all but I wasn't any closer to the team. After training that week, we were running in and the gaffer was way over there, collecting balls or something, and I ran out of my way so I passed him and said, "Gaffer, I'm putting in a transfer request." He just said, "Okay, good lad. You do that." Then I had my agent saying I had to withdraw it because I'd forfeit money but I wasn't interested in money – I just wanted to get moving and play.

'A couple of weeks after that, he put me in the team when we played Huddersfield at home and lost. We were absolutely rubbish. He named the team on the Friday and we'd had all these conversations about me not being in his side and he just said, "Smile, will you?" He gave me an opportunity to stake my claim but mentally I'd already left and I was absolutely crap. It was a horrible way to leave. If I'd sat tight, carried on training well, played in the stiffs and just kept my head down, someone would have come in for me, or I'd have got back in the team and done well.

'But I wasn't a politician. I couldn't just say the right thing. I knew I would say something out of turn eventually. There's never a nice way to leave but that wasn't the way to do it.

'Between Christmas and New Year we went to Barnsley on a Friday night for a game that was on Sky. The gaffer told me David Moyes had rung about me going to Preston and that he'd given them a price and left it with them. He asked if I wanted to travel up for the game. I didn't want to stay at home and wonder what was happening. Anyway, we get to the hotel up in Yorkshire. Sky Sports News is on one of the tellies and it says Preston have signed David Healy, a boy from Manchester United, for a million quid. Well, that was it. The move for me was gone.'

After a couple of loan spells, one at Hibernian and one at Stoke, Smart eventually signed for Oldham Athletic and the nomadic travels of the journeyman footballer continued.

* * *

We met for this interview in a classroom at Brunel University in Uxbridge, where Smart was teaching a group of young footballers, most of them on the books of non-league clubs such as Farnborough, Boreham Wood and St Albans City. Smart was working for a scheme designed to help young players get an alternative career in case football does not take them to where they wanted to go. Smart knows better than most what it takes to survive in the game. It can take you to all corners of the country at the drop of a hat. It can be a precarious living and when it's over there's a lot of life left to live.

When I arrived, he was running a session about safeguarding young people because part of Smart's job was to help them get work experience in the PE departments at schools. The fiery character Smart portrays in some parts of his interview is not apparent in the classroom. Instead he is calm, softly spoken and encouraging. He has the same demeanour on the training ground too, and he has a clear way of explaining what he wants his players to do.

Smart was splitting his time between teaching, coaching and managing Daventry Town in the Southern Premier League Central division.

'It's been a tough ride,' he says. 'When I arrived the playing budget had been cut so I had to get a lot of young lads in. It was hard for them because we had some bad results at times but they learned quickly because they had to. They're getting a chance to play the men's game at a young age and some of them will really benefit from it.'

I ask him whether he tells the teenagers he's teaching or coaching about his own career.

'I don't, really, no. I don't say, "Oh, I scored at Wembley." Some of them are too young to even remember the old Wembley!

'It's funny – they were talking on the radio about the solar eclipse the other day and I remembered the last one, back in 1999. We'd just started the Premier League season and I must've been injured but I was down at Vicarage Road that day. They were doing some building work at the ground and I can remember being there, standing outside the stadium, looking at the solar eclipse through a welder's hat.

'That's where I was. They were talking on the radio about how long it was since the last solar eclipse and to me it does seem so, so long ago now. Sometimes I think to myself, "Bloody hell – did I actually play the game?" Because it feels like another life. It's done and dusted now but it's nice to be reminded about the good times every so often.

'It's always nice to pop down to the club every now and then and I used to go quite regularly, but with managing Daventry that's not something I can do often. I've played in a few charity games for the Watford old boys but my knee is giving me gyp of late and I need an operation on it, but I'm putting it on the back burner.

'To sum it up, though, some of my best days in football, some of the best days of my life, were at Watford, without a doubt.'

9

These days it's not unusual for a team of players born in nine or ten different countries to line up for the Hornets.

Back in the day, of course, it was rare for Watford to have any foreigners.

If you lived through the 1980s, you'll remember how quirky it seemed to have a Dutchman patrolling the midfield.

This is a potted history of Watford's relationship with overseas players and a run through some of the good, the bad, the forgettable and the so-bad-they-were-good…

THE UNITED NATIONS OF WATFORD

Back in September 2012, just a few months after the Pozzo family had taken control of Watford and with the team off to a slow start in the Championship, the backlash was in full swing.

In the *Daily Mail*, under the headline, Why Watford are a snapshot of all that's wrong with the modern game, Martin Samuel wrote: 'The sell is Alexis Sanchez. The reality is Steve Leo Beleck. The fantasy is a brave new world. The reality is 20th in the Championship…

'So who are they, this legion of temporary hired hands? Nobody you would know. Joel Ekstrand, Jean-Alain Fanchone, Neuton, Marco Cassetti, Almen Abdi, Christian Battocchio, Fernando Forestieri, Steve Leo Beleck, Matej Vydra, Alex Geijo, Daniel Pudil, Ikechi Anya, Nathaniel Chalobah, Geoffrey Mujangi Bia. Beautiful British names, as Al Murray's Pub Landlord might say.'

To be fair to Samuel, the main thrust of his argument was that Watford were exploiting a so-called loophole in the rules to bring in a job lot of loan players, primarily from parent club Udinese and the other Pozzo-owned outfit Granada. Of 14 loanees signed that season only one – Chelsea's Sierra Leone-born, English youngster Chalobah – counted towards Watford's 'official' loan quota. By the end of the season, the loophole was closed and the players that Watford wanted to keep were signed permanently.

But it was the last line of Samuel's piece, quoting Al
Murray's parody of the small-minded, xenophobic landlord,
that stood out. The implication was that clubs like Watford had
a responsibility to nurture and develop young British players
and should leave the tricky business of recruiting talent from
abroad to the big boys. Never mind that Chelsea, Arsenal and
Manchester City, among others, had regularly fielded teams full
of players from overseas. Watford, and teams like them, should
know their place and recruit from the lower divisions, where
value-for-money was becoming a thing of the past.

Watford's reputation as a club with a strong youth-team
set-up was established in the 1980s, when they won the FA
Youth Cup twice – in 1982 against Manchester United and
seven years later against Manchester City. The number of players who came through the youth system in the early 1980s
to play a major role in the first team was notable. Kenny
Jackett, Nigel Callaghan, Steve Terry, Nigel Gibbs and Gary
Porter were all members of Tom Walley's youth team and all
made more than 200 appearances for the club, but one of the
examples held up by Samuel as evidence of the club's ability to
nurture future superstars, John Barnes, was not really a product
of that same youth system at all. He was spotted on the playing
fields of north-west London playing for Sudbury Court by a
taxi driver who was friends with one of Watford's scouts. And
although Barnes was capped 79 times by England, he was born
in Kingston, Jamaica.

In the fallow years that followed, Watford's reliance on talent
that emerged from the youth team was largely because it was a
cheaper way to operate. It could also be lucrative if, like Ashley
Young and Marvin Sordell, products of the youth system,
could be sold on for a big profit. But it should also be pointed
out that the ratio of successes to failures has never been as high
as it was in that incredible period in the early 1980s. For every

Ashley Young there's a Dominic Blizzard, a Junior Osbourne and a Joel Grant, plus scores of others who didn't even make it to the first-team.

While plenty of foreign players had represented Watford before, particularly since the late 1990s, the Pozzo era has transformed the club into international operators. Since 2012, there have been a number of firsts – the first Kazakh-born German to play for Watford (Alexander Merkel), the first South Korean (Park Chu-young), the first Romanian (Gabriel Tamas), the first Algerian (Essaïd Belkalem), the first players from Ecuador (Juan Carlos Paredes) and Paraguay (Juan Acuña).

When Watford lost 1-0 at home to Brighton in September 2012, they fielded a starting eleven made up of players born in ten different countries. Jonathan Hogg was the sole Englishman but there was also Irish-born Mark Yeates and Chris Iwelumo, who was born in Coatrbridge, not far from Glasgow. The goalkeeper Manuel Almunia was born in Spain, but was eligible to play for England, had they wanted to select him, because he had spent more than five years in the country and had not been capped by the nation of his birth. Nyron Nosworthy was born in Jamaica. Daniel Pudil and Matej Vydra were both born in Czechoslovakia before it was dissolved and the Czech Republic and Slovakia became countries in their own right. Marco Cassetti was born in Italy. Fernando Forestieri was born in Argentina but had declared for Italy because his parents were Italian. And Almen Abdi was born in Kosovo, which is a disputed territory in the Balkans, and was capped by Switzerland. The cases of Abdi, Forestieri and Almunia, in particular, demonstrate the shifting nature of nationality in football these days.

The notion of eleven local lads representing the town's team only really existed in the very early years of the game because, right from the start of organised football, clubs sought to attract talent from further afield in Britain. Football

is now a global game and the Pozzo network has tentacles
that reach all over the world searching for players who can
improve their teams without breaking the bank.

* * *

The first men born outside Britain and Ireland to play for
the club in a competitive game both made their debut on the
same day in October 1894, in an FA Cup tie against Tottenham
Hotspur. James Oswald Anderson was born in Argentina but
came to England to study, and James Lidderdale was born in
India, where his father worked as a merchant. In the 1950s,
an Australian-born sporting all-rounder called Frank Mitchell
joined Watford after spells at Birmingham City and Chelsea.
Mitchell had moved to England as a teenager and excelled at
both football and cricket, playing for Warwickshire. He ended his football career at Vicarage Road after making himself
popular as a composed, cultured wing-half (these days a position that would be thought of as a midfielder who tended to
go wide, though not an out-and-out winger). A South African
called Roelof Oelofse, better known as Ralph, also joined Watford from Chelsea in the 1950s.

But it wasn't until September 1981 that the first European
player joined Watford. Johannes Hermanus Petrus Lohman,
a tenacious, tough-tackling, left-sided midfielder from the
Netherlands, was recommended to the club by a former
Watford trialist called Paul Kerlin.

Lohman had begun his career with FC Vlaardingen in the
Netherlands, before he moved to Sporting Lokeren in Belgium
where he fell victim to the rule the restricted each club to three
foreign players in their team. At the time, Lohman was one of
seven foreigners at Lokeren and was struggling to get into the
team ahead of Grzegorz Lato and Wlodzimierz Lubanski, who

were both Polish internationals, and the Danish striker Preben Elkjaer Larsen. Lohman went back to Holland on loan for two spells at NEC Nijmegen, who wanted to sign him permanently but could not stump up the fee.

'I had a problem with Lokeren,' said Lohman, who runs a bar in Roosendaal these days. 'They didn't want to sell me to another Belgian club and I was too expensive for Holland. I stopped playing for three months because I couldn't play and I couldn't move. Eventually Lokeren did drop the price but it was too late for Nijmegen because they'd bought two other players. It was just a game to try to get as much money as possible but it didn't work out. I refused to sign another contract with Lokeren so I was automatically suspended by the Belgian Federation.'

Back then, before the Bosman rule changed the way contracts were enforced and transfers were conducted for ever, and for the better, a player could find himself hostage to his club. Although his contract with Lokeren had expired, they still held Lohman's registration and so had great influence over what he could and could not do.

While the dispute was going on, Watford contacted Lohman and invited him for a trial in late August 1981. Lohman was supposed to play a few games in the reserves but because Lokeren still held his registration he was not allowed to.

'I had a training spell for a week and at the end of it they said they would give me a chance,' said Lohman. 'I met Graham Taylor and Elton John on my first trip. It was a very warm welcome and they gave me a really nice feeling about what they wanted.'

Satisfied that Lohman would be an asset for the promotion push towards the First Division, Graham Taylor and chief executive Eddie Plumley flew to Brussels to meet Lokeren's officials and get the deal done. The transfer fee was £25,000, plus £10,000 after Lohman had made a certain number of appearances.

Lohman's first game for the reserves was quite an introduction to English football. The rain at Bristol Rovers was so heavy that the referee considered calling off the game at one point.

Because he had not played regularly since the end of the previous season, it took Lohman time to regain his fitness but, after a couple of months of regular reserve games, he made his first-team debut at home to Charlton Athletic in early December and scored one of the goals in a 2-2 draw. A month later, he scored the only goal of the game to knock Manchester United out of the FA Cup. Because BBC television was easily available in Holland and Belgium, that made Lohman a star in the countries where he had played his football up to that point.

'I had a good start,' he said. 'When I first signed I didn't have a very good contract at all but they were very correct people. They said that if I played a number of games in the first team they would increase my contract. That's what they did after about 10 games. I had already signed for two years so they didn't have to do that but it was very nice.'

Lohman settled in quickly, living with Nigel Callaghan and his parents for the first year and travelling to training with the winger every day. He established himself as a key player as Watford completed their successful push for promotion to the top division.

Foreign players were still a novelty in England at the time. Ipswich had signed accomplished Dutch players Arnold Muhren and Frans Thijssen, who had both had a significant impact, but the general feeling was that they were the exception rather than the rule. Despite England's failures at international level (they didn't even qualify for the World Cup in 1974 or 1978) there was still an attitude that the English game was the best and that foreign players would not adapt to the

pace or competitiveness. Lohman fitted in perfectly, as Graham
Taylor said in his end-of-season assessment, which was
published in the club's official handbook: 'Jan Lohman is
more English than we are in terms of going and winning the
ball. Talk about making contact and going in and winning the
ball fairly – of course this is what he came over here to play
English football for. Dutch football is basically dead, apart
from a couple of clubs, because people are not going to watch
people strolling around and not being really interested in going
in and winning it. What a first season for someone having to
adapt to so much that is new.'

A week after Watford had confirmed promotion with a
2-0 win over Wrexham, Lohman's old club, Sporting Lokeren,
visited Vicarage Road for a friendly that was part of the deal
negotiated to free the player from his contract. Watford played
their usual attacking, high-tempo game with Lohman supporting John Barnes on the left, Nigel Callaghan pinging crosses
in from the right and Luther Blissett and Ross Jenkins causing
havoc in the middle. As the teams came off the pitch at the end
of the game, Wlodzimierz Lubanski, who had scored 48 goals
for the Polish national team, said to Lohman: 'If you can play
with four forwards and go one against one at the back, you
must be some side.'

Lohman wore the number ten shirt in Watford's first-ever
game in the First Division, against Everton in August 1982,
and looked good having got himself into great shape over the
summer. But his season was to be disrupted by injury, which
began a four-year battle with knee problems.

At the start of the following season, Lohman captained the
team and played in Watford's first European tie at Kaiserslautern in West Germany, where he had a goal disallowed. 'I hit it
from well outside the box but the referee disallowed it for offside against Richard Jobson,' he said. He did score in the next

league match, a 4-0 win at Stoke City, but towards the end of
the game he got a kick on the knee. He didn't think too much
of it at first but it got worse and by the time he played the following week, against Spurs at Vicarage Road, he was struggling
badly. That Spurs game, which the visitors won 3-2, is famous
for Glenn Hoddle's sublime chip from the edge of the penalty area that flew over goalkeeper Steve Sherwood's head. The
goal was shown as part of Match of the Day's opening credits
for a few years afterwards. 'I wasn't too pleased with that,' said
Lohman. 'Hoddle did me and then clipped it over Sherwood.'

But it was the knee injury that was causing more concern. 'I
played the Spurs game and it was getting worse and worse,' he
said. 'Then I had a fitness test for Kaiserslautern [the second
leg at home] and I couldn't make it. I could hardly run.

It was 15 months before he returned to the first team briefly,
then he missed the best part of another year. His last goal for
Watford was in a 3-2 home defeat against Liverpool in January
1986, which was televised. A couple of months later, he played
his final game, in a 1-1 FA Cup draw at Bury. At the end of
the season, he was given a free transfer and moved back to
Belgium.

Lohman's stay at Watford was blighted by three knee opera-
tions and the lengthy recovery periods but he must go down in
history as the first European to play for the club at a time when
overseas players were a rarity.

* * *

There was quite a buzz of excitement when it emerged that the
United States' World Cup goalkeeper Tony Meola was training
with the Hornets in the autumn of 1990. The USA were not
exactly a footballing powerhouse at the time, and Meola had
conceded five in a 5-1 defeat in their opening game at Italia '90,

but these were barren days for Watford and Colin Lee's team had got off to a shocking start to the season. The talented teenager David James was between the sticks but there was still a sense that he might be a bit too green to be first-choice through the whole campaign and so the opportunity to give a trial to a player with international experience made sense.

Meola was born in New Jersey. His father had played for Avellino in the Italian second division before emigrating to the States and Meola had been a talented sportsman at school and college, excelling at baseball, basketball and soccer. He eventually settled on goalkeeping and, once established as the national team's number one, he headed to England to try to get a contract.

Before the World Cup he'd had a brief spell at Sheffield Wednesday and then started the 1990-91 season at Brighton, where he made his Football League debut only to be released shortly afterwards. He spent a couple of months training with Watford and was then handed a chance, in a home Full Members Cup tie against Bristol Rovers. He made a bit of a hash of one of the Rovers chances and conceded a sloppy goal in a 2-1 defeat and he was let go. Four years later, Meola starred as the USA goalkeeper and captain as they reached the second round of their home World Cup, losing to eventual champions, Brazil.

It was not until the late 1990s, when Graham Taylor returned as manager, that Watford began to cast their net further afield for foreign talent. The Premier League had begun to attract some of the world's top stars but Taylor realised that clever recruitment from overseas could save a club money and so he engaged a number of scouts to keep an eye on European leagues. Foreign players were not a familiar sight in the lower divisions at the time and it is fair to say that there were more misses than hits.

Of course Ronny Rosenthal, the Israeli forward, was well-known in England, having joined Liverpool from Standard Liège in Belgium before moving on to Tottenham. Rosenthal's successful spell at Vicarage Road is covered in volume three of this series but it was he who recommended Taylor take a look at his compatriot – an elegant, upright and composed midfielder called Alon Hazan, who arrived in January 1998 and played a bit-part role in two successive promotions.

At the start of the Second Division promotion campaign, Taylor brought in a Seattle-born Danish right-back called Lars Melvang, who scored on his debut against Brentford, endured a torrid time against Swindon's pacy but past-his-best winger Mark Walters in the very next game, made another three appearances and then disappeared again. Melvang had plenty of experience, having won the Danish title with both Odense and Silkeborg, but he was no Nigel Gibbs – the man he was ostensibly brought in to replace.

Later that season, another Scandinavian full-back arrived, although you probably won't remember the name Per-Ola Ljung, even if you were one of a few hardy souls who made the midweek December evening trip to Craven Cottage to watch a Watford reserve side lose 1-0 to Fulham in the Auto Wind-screens Shield. Ljung was no spring chicken – he'd just turned 30 and had played more than 400 games for Helsingborgs in the Swedish league – and that Fulham match was his only appearance for Watford.

In 1998-99, Taylor took a few more calculated gambles. He signed Michel Ngonge on the strength of a video compilation that made him look like Pele. Ngonge was born in Huy in the Belgian Ardennes and played for the Democratic Republic of Congo. He'd bumped around the Belgian leagues before joining Samsunspor in Turkey. After a couple of years there, he came to Watford's attention and Taylor snapped him up for free when the Turkish club left him unpaid for two months. While not the most refined footballer, he was energetic, quick and unpredictable, which caused defenders a headache. He scored on his debut, against Bradford City, and again three days later in a League Cup tie at Cambridge and, although he wasn't prolific (he only scored four more that season), he forced his way into the team just in time for the play-offs and scored the only goal in the semi-final first-leg win over Birmingham.

The Premier League was probably a bit too much for him but he did score in the opening game of the 1999-2000 season at home to Wimbledon, and also found the net in three consecutive games – against Sheffield Wednesday, Newcastle and Sunderland – in November. Ngonge went on loan to Huddersfield shortly after that and moved to QPR at the end of the season but of the foreign players Taylor took a chance on during the First Division promotion season, his was the most significant contribution.

An Icelandic midfielder called Johann Gudmundsson scored twice on his debut – a 2-2 draw with Port Vale – but didn't really make the grade. Nigeria's World Cup full-back Ben Iroha looked the real deal but was afflicted by a nasty case of bunions and got an infection after an operation to treat them, which forced him to retire. Alexandre Bonnot was a small but handy midfielder who, on first glance, looked like he wished the game was played at a slower pace but who possessed a neat touch to find himself the time he needed to pick out a good pass. But with the partnership between Micah Hyde and Richard Johnson so strong, the Frenchman found opportunities restricted.

* * *

The first season in the Premiership saw four European players arrive, to wildly differing effect. Barrel-chested midfielder Adrian Bakalli trundled onto the pitch as a substitute at Leicester

City early on and stood in the centre of the park looking like he'd just wandered into the living room but couldn't remember for the life of him what for. In September, a Dutch winger called Nordin Wooter arrived from Real Sociedad for just short of a million pounds and looked brilliant on his debut, a 1-0 win against Chelsea. But he failed to capture those heights again in his subsequent couple of seasons – apart from a brilliant mazy run that took him past the entire Norwich team before scoring a memorable goal.

As winter set in, and Taylor grasped at straws to try to keep the team afloat, the opportunity to sign Xavier Gravelaine presented itself and the manager thought, 'What have I got to lose?'

Gravelaine was the epitome of the mercurial number ten who could be devastatingly brilliant when he fancied turning it on but who skulked into the shadows when the mood took him. Speaking to some of his team-mates provokes the same response – a roll of the eyes. Some suggest he only came to Vicarage Road for the money, most describe him as a 'weird bloke' and the list of clubs he'd played for in France was as long as his arm. He rarely stayed anywhere long – two years at Marseille was his longest stint – which perhaps gives a hint at his personality.

He scored two great goals in a rare win over Southampton at Christmas time but may as well not have been on the pitch for the rest of his brief stay at Watford. There was undoubtedly a language barrier, although Taylor describes him as one of those players who understood English well enough when the praise was being handed out but seemed to have problems comprehending the criticism.

One day during training, frustrated at the difficulty getting his message across and infuriated by Gravelaine's refusal to do the tracking-back and closing-down work Taylor required of his front men, the manager asked Frenchman Alex Bonnot to translate some instructions.

Gravelaine, who had a dark-eyed stare that suggested a short fuse, and a temper that confirmed it, listened as Bonnot translated Taylor's words.

The training match continued and Gravelaine played in the same casual manner, only running when there was a shot on goal to be had, refusing to muck in and defend from the front.

So Taylor asked Bonnot to repeat the message. Still no response.

At the end of the session, Bonnot went to the manager to have a quiet word and admitted that instead of translating Taylor's instructions to chase, harry and generally work his socks off, he had told Gravelaine that the manager thought he was doing fine and to carry on as he was. Bonnet admitted that telling his temperamental compatriot to put a shift in didn't appeal too much and Taylor had to laugh.

Things came to a head with a bit of a training-ground row during a brief winter break to Portugal. Kenny Jackett told Gravelaine to get out of his sight and that's exactly what the Frenchman did. He left as suddenly as he'd arrived, his contract was cancelled and he turned out for another half a dozen teams before retiring in 2004.

If Gravelaine could justifiably be described as work shy on the football pitch, his successor in the Watford forward line was the complete opposite. Icelandic striker Heidar Helguson, who came from Norwegian club Lillestrom for a new club record fee of £1.5million, was as whole-hearted as they come. Taylor had to move quickly to sign Helguson in January 2000 because he knew several other English clubs, including Gordon Strachan's Coventry, were circling.

Helguson quickly became a fans' favourite and is – to date, anyway – the only foreign player to have been inducted into the

Hornets hall of fame. His commitment, desire and willingness to put his head and body in among the boots and elbows was the key to his popularity as much as his goals. The fans had a chance to restate their affection for him when he returned for a lengthy loan spell in late 2009.

* * *

And so, we move into the modern era of the 'have boots, will travel' footballer. It has to be said that the 2000s saw very patchy recruitment of foreign players – and most of those who did arrive at Vicarage Road had at least been tested elsewhere in England first. Allan Nielsen, another record signing – the first to break the £2million barrier – had been a qualified success at Tottenham but served Watford with distinction, running the team's midfield like a stoker keeping the fires burning through sheer sweat and hard work.

Another arrival from Tottenham, Ramon Vega, was among the flops signed by Gianluca Vialli, although the Italian manager must also take great credit for giving us the opportunity to see first-hand the classy defending of Filippo Galli, who had previously starred for Milan. Then again, Patrick Blondeau has to be considered in the case against Vialli, too, as does Pierre Issa, who at least gave us something to remember him by when he fell off a stretcher while being carried off injured.

As the decade moved on, the sight of foreign players in a Watford shirt became less exotic. Brynjar Gunnarsson was another Icelandic player who did well; Jay DeMerit left North America for the English non-league and made it all the way to the Premier League. Tamas Priskin, the Slovak-born Hungarian striker, flattered to deceive but then redeemed himself by moving to Ipswich for a vastly-inflated transfer fee; Collins John, the Liberian striker, was expensive and instantly forgettable.

When the team's fortunes faded, so Watford picked up players on loan or on free transfers who had done well elsewhere in England, such as the goalkeepers Mart Poom of Latvia and Tomasz Kuszcazk of Poland, or the Polish striker Grezgorz Rasiak or Swedish winger Alex Kacaniklic. In the case of the loanees, these were players Watford fans could only dream of signing at the time, and when their clubs did decide to let them go, they moved elsewhere.

* * *

With the arrival of the Pozzos, Watford were plugged into a 100-strong pool of talent gathered from all over the world. Suddenly, every new signing came with a pronunciation guide and the wider footballing world wrote the team off as a bunch of 'Italian' misfits.

That, of course, sells short the melting pot of cultures and nationalities that Watford now represents. This became a team where an Algerian-born Frenchman could pass to a Mexican who could cross it for an Italian to lay back for an Englishman to fire into the roof of the net.

Aside from observing the rules over the number of 'home grown' players they can field, nationality is almost an irrelevance these days. Everybody in a yellow shirt plays for the flag of Watford and runs out to our equivalent of the national anthem, Z-Cars. And, of course, as the team stepped onto the biggest stage in world football, we knew there would be people all over the globe following the Hornets' fortunes – whether it's supporters of Udinese and Granada keen to see how their brothers are getting on, or Miguel Layun's 1.8million Twitter followers in Mexico (more followers than Tottenham Hotspur, by the way) hoping for a glimpse of their man.

Either way, Watford are global now.

10

If you were to pick your all-time
Watford team, it would be a surprise
if the name John McClelland were not
included at the heart of the defence.

Even if you are too young to have seen
the Northern Irishman wear the
number six shirt for the Hornets, his
place in the hall of fame and his
record during five years at Vicarage
Road warrant selection.

McClelland was the man who came in
and calmed down an erratic defence
and made himself into a terrace
favourite.

You could almost say he made the job
of defending into an art form…

THE ART OF DEFENDING

John McClelland was the third player to be inducted into the Hornets hall of fame, after all-time top scorer Luther Blissett and one of the club's finest goalkeepers, Tony Coton. It is a subjective statement but the Northern Irishman was arguably the best central defender ever to play for Watford and would surely be one of the first names on the teamsheet if you were to pick an all-time side.

He joined Watford in November 1984, a month before his 29th birthday, and his impact on the team was immediate as he steadied a young but talented defence that was prone to attacks of the wobbles with his calm approach.

The previous season, Watford had reached the FA Cup final and fielded a very young back four at Wembley. This was partly forced upon the manager, Graham Taylor, because the left-back and captain Wilf Rostron was suspended, but the defence that faced Everton consisted of 20-year-old Neil Price (Rostron's replacement), 19-year-old David Bardsley on the opposite flank with 18-year-old Lee Sinnott and the daddy of them all, 21-year-old Steve Terry, in the centre.

With another central defender, Steve Sims, moving to Notts County in the summer, Watford were short of experience at the back and as the 1984-85 season got underway, it showed.

They kept just one clean sheet in the opening 16 league and cup matches – that was in a 4-0 win at Leeds United in the Milk Cup. But the most concerning thing was the number of goals

Watford were conceding. In the first three months of the season, Watford lost 4-3 at home to Arsenal, lost 3-2 at Norwich and Luton, drew 3-3 with Aston Villa, Newcastle and Ipswich and, worst of the lot, lost 5-4 to Everton at Vicarage Road.

You couldn't say it wasn't exciting. Watford were scoring enough to win games but the grand total in the goals against column – 32 from just 13 matches – meant the team were second from bottom in the First Division.

That extraordinary defeat to the Toffees was Tony Coton's debut following his £300,000 move from Birmingham City and it confirmed to Taylor that the problem wasn't between the posts. He needed someone who could add a bit of steel to the defence, someone who could organise the team from the back.

The man Taylor wanted was the captain of Glasgow Rangers and there was a chance he might be able to sign McClelland because the player and his club were locked in a lengthy dispute over his contract.

PLAYING FOR GLASGOW RANGERS

McClelland's career had taken him all over the place, from Portadown in Northern Ireland to Cardiff City and Bangor in Wales, Mansfield Town in the Fourth Division and then, in 1981, to Glasgow Rangers. Three years into his career at Ibrox, he had played for Northern Ireland at the 1982 World Cup in Spain and been appointed captain of his club, but he felt Rangers were going back on a promise they'd made when they signed him from Mansfield.

Billy Bingham had been sacked by Mansfield and had taken over as Northern Ireland manager and called McClelland up to the national team as a utility player. McClelland played in a central midfield role in a match against Scotland at Hampden Park in May 1981 and, while still at the hotel in Glasgow, he got a call from someone at Mansfield saying, 'We've sold you to Glasgow Rangers. They're going to come and pick you up to take you to Ibrox to sort out your contract.'

'I asked them what the transfer fee was,' says McClelland, picking up the story. 'They told me it was £100,000, which was not bad money considering they got me from non-league for £10,000. Anyway, I thought that I'd get 10 per cent of the transfer fee as a signing-on fee, because I thought that was what happened, but Mansfield said, "No, talk to Rangers about that."

'I met the Rangers manager, John Greig, at Ibrox and it was quite intimidating because he took me up the marble staircase and into the oak-panelled room where I was given a silver-service meal. I said, "Before we start, am I going to get 10 per cent of the transfer fee?"

'John Greig said, "I'm very disappointed in you, John. The first thing you want to talk about is money."

'I was sinking down in my seat thinking, "Oh dear, this isn't a very good start." But I said that if I signed I wanted a signing-on fee. Greig replied that money shouldn't be my God and blah, blah, blah. He said that I was just starting out and that Rangers were giving me this amazing chance to progress. They told me I had to get in the team and prove myself first.

'I was on £120 a week at Mansfield and Rangers offered me £200 a week. I said that Mansfield were in the Fourth Division, playing in front of 5,000 people, and Rangers were in the top division in Scotland playing in front of 30,000 people. They were paying £100,000 for an international footballer. They said they knew I was living okay on £120 a week in Mansfield and that I'd be living very well on £200 in Glasgow. They offered a three-year contract and said that once I'd proved myself it would all change. The choice was simple, did I want to play for Mansfield or Glasgow Rangers?'

So McClelland signed for three years with Rangers and the

following summer went to the World Cup in Spain not expecting to be a first choice.

PLAYING IN THE WORLD CUP

'I didn't realise at the time what it all meant because we were just working hard to make sure we didn't lose every game 5-0,' says McClelland of the 1982 World Cup. 'I played in a few warm-up games and I felt I was doing well but I was still surprised when Billy Bingham put me in for the first game. I did well and I kept my place.'

Northern Ireland drew their opening two games – 0-0 against Yugoslavia and 1-1 against Honduras – and faced the hosts, Spain, in the final match. Because of the way the group had worked out, Northern Ireland knew that a 2-2 draw or a 1-0 win would mean both they and Spain went through at Yugoslavia's expense, but a 1-1 draw would see the Irish go out.

'We didn't score many goals but we were very well organised and, tactically, good at stopping people. We knew if we could keep it tight we might have a chance to get a goal,' McClelland says.

And that's exactly what happened. Watford's striker Gerry Armstrong stunned the Spanish and when Mal Donaghy was sent off for the Irish, McClelland and his team-mates had their backs against the wall to cling on to the lead.

'It was so hot we knew we couldn't go charging about for 90 minutes, so we concentrated on stopping the danger before it became a problem, which is the best way to defend anyway.'

Northern Ireland was bitterly split between Catholics and Protestants but the national team seemed to transcend that divide. McClelland had never truly fitted into either camp anyway because his mother was a Catholic and his father was a Protestant. The team's success in the World Cup – they qualified for the second group phase, which was effectively the quarter-final round – smoothed tensions for a few weeks that summer. 'At the time there were people getting killed every week in Northern Ireland but during the World Cup there was no trouble at all. The police said they wished the World Cup was on all the time,' he says.

LEAVING RANGERS

When McClelland returned for pre-season with Rangers, John Greig made him the captain. 'He said I'd come back from the World Cup a different player,' McClelland says. And yet he was still on £200 a week until his contract expired in the summer of 1984.

'I played virtually every game for Rangers,' he says. 'I missed only one game because I was sent off but when my contract ended all they were prepared to offer me was another £50 a week. I asked if there was a bonus for signing on again and they said that they only offered signing-on fees to new players. I said, "I didn't get a signing-on fee when I joined." They said, "Well, you've missed the boat then."

McClelland felt he was being taken advantage of and his reluctance to sign a new contract did not go down too well. 'There were stories in the press saying I was holding the club to ransom and all this but I didn't feel it was fair.'

In the days before the Bosman ruling changed the transfer system for ever, McClelland was stuck because Rangers held his registration. He couldn't just sign for another club, Rangers were entitled to a transfer fee even though McClelland was not under contract.

'It was an anomaly that wasn't right,' says McClelland. 'But I think it's now gone the other way and now it's not right for a club who develops a player and then could lose him for nothing at the end of his contract. So we've gone from one bad system to another bad system.'

JOINING WATFORD

Graham Taylor travelled to see Rangers play in the Scottish League Cup final at the end of October and found himself sitting next to Arsenal manager Don Howe. Taylor asked Howe who he had his eye on. 'John McClelland,' said Howe. 'But he's playing out of position so I'm not too sure.'

McClelland played left-back in that game and Taylor was quietly delighted to see him playing out of position but knew he must move quickly to get his man.

A week or so later, McClelland played centre forward for Rangers in a UEFA Cup tie against Inter Milan and after the game he had a couple of meetings set up at a hotel near the airport.

In one room were Graham Taylor and Watford's chief executive Eddie Plumley, On the same floor, three doors along and on the opposite side of the corridor waited Aberdeen manager Alex Ferguson and his secretary.

'I said to Graham, "I don't want to mess about. You make me an offer and I'll say yes or no." They offered me £500 a week and a signing-on fee which was to be paid over the duration of a four-and-a-half year contract. I was happy with that but said I wanted to go and meet Aberdeen out of courtesy to say no to them.

'Graham and Eddie were very anxious that I signed the contract before I went to see Aberdeen because they were worried I'd change my mind but I had decided what I wanted to do. I wanted to get out of Scotland. I refused to sign the contract but gave Graham my word. I felt that it would show him that I was a man of my word.'

McClelland walked across the corridor to see Ferguson.

'We were having a cup of tea and a biscuit and after the small talk, Fergie said, "We've won the league, we're in Europe, we've got the oil and the money, we'll have the best defence in Scotland with Alex McLeish and John McClelland."

'He wrote down a number on a piece of paper, folded it and slid it across the table to me. He said, "I don't know what Watford are offering you but they'll not get close to that."

'I said, "I'm sorry, but I'm not going to look at it." Fergie was trying to get me to look at it and I said, "It's not been about money, it's been about respect and shaking hands on something. I have decided to go to England and if I look at that and sign for you, you'll think I'm a mercenary. If I don't look at it, at least you can't say I'm a greedy footballer."'

'I'll be honest, I'd have done anything to get out of Rangers at that time so if it hadn't been Graham, it would have been someone else, but I'd always heard good things from Gerry Armstrong about Watford. Often when you join up with the international side there's a few players whinging about what's going on at their club but I never heard anything but positive things about Graham.'

Three days after playing for Rangers in Europe against Inter, McClelland made his First Division debut for Watford against Sunderland, following a transfer that cost £225,000.

Acutely aware of Watford's poor start to the season, Taylor's programme notes for that afternoon's game were headlined: 'Don't Panic.'

That could almost be McClelland's motto. Everything he says is underpinned by an air of calmness. 'I looked at Watford's results and saw that they were scoring lots of goals,' he says. 'There's not too much wrong if Luther Blissett and John Barnes are hitting the net. To me, that's the hardest part of the game. All I had to do was help organise the team so the ball didn't go in that eight yard by eight foot frame. That's the easy bit – I find, anyway.'

Having conceded 32 in 13 – a rate of 2.46 goals against per game – Watford's defence improved with McClelland in the side. They conceded 39 in the remaining 29 games – a rate of 1.34 per game. That might not be the most parsimonious defensive record in the history of the game but Watford's style of play was based on trying to outscore the opposition, rather than keep everything tight. As McClelland says: 'Graham said he knew we'd concede one a game but we were capable of scoring more than that so we could cope with that.'

Watford had been 21st in the table when McClelland joined. They finished the season 11th and McClelland was named player of the season. 'I was a bit embarrassed about that, coming to the club in November and winning the award because the forward players did the difficult bit, the creative bit. Being organised and stopping the opposition was just what I did.'

APPEARANCES CAN BE DECEPTIVE

McClelland's new team-mates were not immediately impressed when they saw him hobble out onto the training ground after completing his medical, the day before he made his debut. At first glance he never looked the most mobile of players and he walked in a way that could be almost mistaken for a limp. But there was a moment in the game against Sunderland where he accelerated to dispossess their forward Howard Gayle, who was no slouch. For a moment it had looked like Sunderland were about to score, until McClelland intervened and passed the ball back to Coton.

Steve Terry turned to McClelland and said: 'Are you really that quick?'

McClelland said: 'I guess so. Can you head a ball?'

Terry replied: 'Yes.'

McClelland said: 'I think we're going to be alright then.'

'I suppose I had that look about me,' McClelland says. 'I was easy to underestimate. When I was at Bangor, we were playing in the Welsh Cup final against Wrexham and the manager got us all in a room and went through their team man by man, telling us what they were good at, what they were bad at. By the time he got to the number nine, my man, I was asleep. The manager wasn't too happy about that but the other players said, "Don't worry about John, he'll be alright."

'Years later, I invited a load of my old Bangor team-mates to watch me play for Watford at Liverpool and one of the old pros said, "You're still doing that old trick of pretending to be dopey, then?"

'It was a bit like Columbo pretending to be daft. It wasn't really a deliberate thing but when I realised it was what I did, I used it to my advantage.

'Steve Harrison, who was Watford's defensive coach when I joined, told me a story about one of my early games. They could hear the conversation on the opposing team's bench and someone was saying, "I don't know what's wrong with our number nine today but he can't even outrun that old fella McClelland." That would happen on a regular basis. Because I didn't look a certain way, or run a certain way, it was easy to assume I couldn't play.'

THE ART OF DEFENDING

McClelland played for Watford during the most consistently successful era in the club's history. After promotion in 1982, European competition in 1983 and the FA Cup final in 1984, Graham Taylor was seeking to establish the club in the top half of the First Division. At the end of McClelland's first season, 1984-85, Watford finished 11th. They then finished 12th and ninth before Taylor left to join Aston Villa in the summer of 1987. In those two seasons, the team conceded 62 and 54 league goals. In 1987-88, when Dave Bassett replaced Taylor as manager, Watford were relegated but McClelland was voted player of the season for a second time. The team's problems were at the other end of the pitch that season. They simply couldn't score enough goals – managing only 27 – but they were relatively solid at the back, conceding only 51, which was the 10th best defensive record in the division that season.

But what was it about McClelland that made him such an outstanding defender? 'When I was 40, I signed for Darlington as a coach and my wife said to me, "Don't go thinking you're young enough to play!" I said, "Don't worry, I'm going to be a coach."

'Then one day, the manager, Jim Platt, took me to one side and said he wanted to play me in the first-team. I told him it wasn't a good idea because if I played badly, they'd slaughter him for playing a 40-year-old and if I played well, they'd say the same thing.

'But Jim wanted me to go in alongside the young lads. He didn't say anything else to me before the game but in the team talk he said to the other players, "John knows where the danger is coming from, so just listen to what he tells you. Just listen."

'And that's what I could do. I did know where the danger would come from. Graham Taylor recognised where goals were scored from and the majority of goals come from the same areas, often as a result of defensive mistakes. So I always did the things that would limit mistakes and reduce the number of chances the opposition had to score.

'My rules of defending, the rules I lived by, have never changed. Certain things in football don't change. There might be more money, the speed of the game might be quicker but the rules of football have not changed and that means the job of defending is still the same 30 years on.

'When I see defenders breaking 'my' rules, I can tell a goal is going to be scored. I see it on Match of the Day every Saturday night. I'm a bit like Alan Hansen in that I see the bad defending before I see the good attacking.

'Don't get me wrong, there are some very clever players who can do special things and sometimes you just have to live with that. Sometimes the opposition is better than you but goals still come from the same areas. They come when the ball and the forward get into a position where the defender is not between them and the goal.

'To me, time and space are the same thing. If I drop off my attacker by three yards, that gives me a second-and-a-half to think. If I am standing right up next to the centre forward, and I'm our last man, then I haven't got any time to think because all I can do is react to the danger when it happens. If the ball comes over the top, I'm in a running race with the forward, whereas if I drop off and anticipate what's going to happen I have a better chance of covering. So, being tight to your forward doesn't necessarily mean you're defending well.

'But anticipating danger is one thing as long as you don't try to be too clever. I remember playing for Watford, against West Brom, I learned something. I was marking Imre Varadi and as the ball was played up from the back to their other centre forward I guessed that the centre forward was going to flick it on just as Varadi was making his run. So I stepped up, thinking I'd play Varadi offside. Unfortunately, the centre forward missed it, as did Steve Terry, and it went past me to Varadi, who scored. I had assumed something would happen but it didn't, so it taught me not to get too clever.'

Of the defenders McClelland played with at Watford, he was impressed by Wilf Rostron, the left-back and captain, because he could read the game so well and he later struck up an excellent partnership with Steve Sims, who made a surprise return to the club in 1986 after a couple years away. 'Simsy's legs may not have been as quick as they'd been earlier in his career but he knew the game inside out and together we could keep a tight ship. I was quick, so I could make up for other people's mistakes.

'I couldn't handle forward players who couldn't think. The top players have all been taught the game and so when you go up against them, it's like a game of chess where you're trying to outwit each other. I remember we played Walsall in the FA Cup three times because we drew with them twice. They had a little forward called David Cross. I really couldn't get to grips with him and at the end of the third game, even though we'd won, I said, "You get to take me home and put me on your mantelpiece now," because he caused me a lot of problems. I am not being disrespectful but some of the hardest players to play against were the ones who didn't know what they were going to do next, so you couldn't read them.

'Gary Lineker, for example, was a great goalscorer because he knew where to run. So when I marked him there was no point me trying to out-think him. He knew where the goals were because he scored 30 of them every year, so I let him dictate. I let him move and I went with him. That's how to play against Lineker and players like him. Use what they are good at against them. He's going to make his runs and you're not going to be able to stop him doing what he wants to do, so follow him and don't let him get goal-side of you.

'I say to kids now – there are 22 players on the pitch and you play for 90 minutes. If you think about it, when you take off time for stoppages, throw-ins and all that, each player is involved with the ball for about three minutes. So, that means you are without the ball for 87 minutes.

'My game was all about doing the right thing when I didn't have the ball – which was most of the time. I was constantly asking myself the same questions, "Where am I? Am I in the right position? Are my team-mates in the right position."

'The biggest danger is actually when our team had the ball because that's when everyone gets sucked in to following the ball instead of concentrating on their position and the player they should be marking. So I would think, "If we lose the ball now, are we in the right position to defend?"

'I'd be asking those questions and making small adjustments every five seconds of every game. And I'd be talking to my other defenders, especially the younger ones. "Go there... that's far enough. Okay, come closer to me..."

'Back in Northern Ireland someone once said to me, "I've never seen someone influence the game so much by doing so little." It was a nice thing to say but really I was working all the time on our defensive positions.

'Of course, forwards can do something special but you just have to take those on the chin. And you can make mistakes but, fortunately, I made relatively few mistakes.'

One such mistake was against Arsenal in the 1987 FA Cup quarter-final, which gave the Gunners the opening goal, although Watford went on to win the tie 3-1.

'The ball was going through to the goalkeeper and Tony [Coton] shouted for it but the pitch was heavy and I wasn't sure it would carry through to him. The Arsenal forward was right on my shoulder, so I tried to take it away from him but Ian Allinson nipped in and scored. It was my mistake and I put my hands up straight away, "That's my fault, lads." Tony called it but I didn't let it run back to him.

'Often defenders don't want to admit their mistakes but there's no point trying to say otherwise when it's your fault. I think your team-mates trust you more, and respect you more, if you're honest when it's your fault.

'I was usually calm after incidents like that because I thought, "Well, I don't make many mistakes so if that's my one, I should be okay for the next five or six games." But I see a lot of centre halves try to over-compensate when they make a mistake by going in harder or trying to be more decisive. I think they play themselves into more trouble that way. But if that was the right way for them to play, why weren't they playing like that in the first place? You have to stick to the basics, stay calm and carry on playing the percentages – because that's what it is all about. It's a fact of life that a football team is going to concede goals. Even Barcelona concede goals – okay, not as many as most teams, but they still let some in. So you are playing the percentages all the time, working to cut out as many possible chances as you can.'

McClelland is adamant that his golden rules are as valid now as they were when he played. 'When your team haven't got the ball, keep yourself between the man you are marking and the goal. If he's the goal side of you and the ball comes to him, he's got a chance to score. When the man you are marking has got the ball, keep yourself between the ball and the goal.

'It sounds simple but with so much movement going on in a game, it can be easy to get distracted and get pulled out of position, so it takes a lot of concentration and discipline but as a defender, that's your job.

'As I said, you can play a game of football for 90 minutes and spend less than three minutes in total in the vicinity of the ball. A lot of my touches on the ball might be heading it clear or kicking it clear. It's not necessarily glamorous but if you switch off and stop doing the basic things well, you can cost your team a goal in the blink of an eye.'

McClelland left Watford at the end of the unsuccessful push for promotion back to the top flight in 1988-89. He limped off in his final game – the second leg of a frustrating play-off semi-final against Blackburn Rovers. Watford drew 0-0 away and 1-1 at home and were eliminated on away goals, the only time an undefeated team has been knocked out of the play-offs. At the start of that season, he had turned down an approach from Manchester United when Alex Ferguson wanted to sign him to bolster their defence. 'My view was that I'd been part of the team that was relegated so it was my duty to try to get them promoted again,' says McClelland.

He moved to Leeds United but returned to Vicarage Road briefly on loan the following season and made one appearance. Then he played enough games for Leeds to earn a medal when the Elland Road club won the First Division title in 1992 – the last season before it became the Premier League.

But it was at Watford where he played most of his football – making 184 appearances in five years. In 1987, his consistency was recognised when he was selected by England manager Bobby Robson as part of a Football League team to face Diego Maradona and a star-studded Rest of the World side when the Football League celebrated its 100th anniversary at Wembley.

Much of the time his reassuring presence at the back was perhaps taken for granted. The potential dangers he snuffed out by doing the simple, almost invisible things, was not going to excite the crowd, although his efforts were certainly appreciated by the Watford supporters, as two player of the season awards prove.

'When I left Watford, someone wrote a letter to me, which eventually found its way to me after I'd moved house,' he says. 'The letter said, "I used to go and watch Watford with my son and I thought defending was boring. But you have made it an art form and I like watching it." I thought that was a nice thing to say. Anyway, when you're a defender you don't want to draw attention to yourself by making a mistake, do you?'